Common Core Mastery

Reading
Paired Text

Grade **2**

The following images were provided through Shutterstock.com and are protected by copyright:
Picsfive, GVictoria (page 64); Jarous (pages 64, 66); Pete Spiro, Neveshkin Nikolay, Melinda Dawyer, Feng Yu (page 69); Chupi, anaken2012, Critterbiz (page 104); sritangphoto, Gerry Boughan, Steve Lovegrove (page 116); Ammentorp Photography (page 124); Peter Sobolev, Iryna Denysova, Ken Wolter (page 156); Tom Gowanlock, Stephen Griffith (page 164)

Permissions for the remaining images were provided by the organizations and individuals listed below:
Crazy Horse Memorial (pages 105, 106); Dorothea Lange (page 117); Russell Lee (page 124); Dick DeMarsico (page 125); U.S. National Archives and Records Administration (page 126)

Editorial Development: Guadalupe Lopez
Lisa Vitarisi Mathews
Copy Editing: Laurie Westrich
Art Direction: Cheryl Puckett
Cover Design: Yuki Meyer
Cover Illustration: Chris Vallo
Illustration: Mary Rojas
Design/Production: Susan Lovell
Jessica Onken
Art & Photo Management: Kathy Kopp

EMC 1372

Evan-Moor
Helping Children Learn

Visit
teaching-standards.com
to view a correlation
of this book.
This is a free service.

*Correlated to State and
Common Core State Standards*

**Congratulations on your purchase of some of the
finest teaching materials in the world.**

*Photocopying the pages in this book
is permitted for single-classroom use only.
Making photocopies for additional classes
or schools is prohibited.*

For information about other Evan-Moor products, call 1-800-777-4362,
fax 1-800-777-4332, or visit our Web site, www.evan-moor.com.
Entire contents © 2014 EVAN-MOOR CORP.
18 Lower Ragsdale Drive, Monterey, CA 93940-5746. Printed in USA.

CPSIA: Printed by McNaughton & Gunn, Saline, MI USA. [1/2014]

Contents

Corrections
Common Core State Standards

	Science Selections							
RIT Reading Standards for Informational Text, Grade 2	Apple Tree Swing	Parts of an Apple	Jack's Wheels	Six Simple Machines	What Will a Magnet Attract?	Magnificent Magnets	Stone Soup	Mexican Wedding Cakes
Key Ideas and Details								
2.1 Ask and answer such questions as *who*, *what*, *where*, *when*, *why*, and *how* to demonstrate understanding of key details in a text.		●		●	●			
2.2 Identify the main topic of a multiparagraph text as well as the focus of specific paragraphs within the text.		●		●	●			
2.3 Describe the connection between a series of historical events, scientific ideas or concepts, or steps in technical procedures in a text.		●		●	●			
Craft and Structure								
2.4 Determine the meaning of words and phrases in a text relevant to a grade 2 topic or subject area.		●		●	●			
2.5 Know and use various text features (e.g., captions, bold print, subheadings, glossaries, indexes, electronic menus, icons) to locate key facts or information in a text efficiently.		●		●	●			
2.6 Identify the main purpose of a text, including what the author wants to answer, explain, or describe.		●		●	●			
Integration of Knowledge and Ideas								
2.7 Explain how specific images (e.g., a diagram showing how a machine works) contribute to and clarify a text.		●		●	●			
2.8 Describe how reasons support specific points the author makes in a text.		●		●	●			
Range of Reading and Level of Text Complexity								
2.10 By the end of the year, read and comprehend informational texts, including history/social studies, science, and technical texts, in the grades 2–3 text complexity band proficiently, with scaffolding as needed at the high end of the range.		●		●	●			

Reading Paired Text • EMC 1372 • © Evan-Moor Corp.

Correlations
Common Core State Standards

Social Studies Selections									Reading Standards for Informational Text, Grade 2
Mount Rushmore	Colossal Crazy Horse	Chavez and the Grape Boycott	King and the Bus Boycott	Railroad Songs	Tracks Across America	Farm Art	Wall of Welcome	**RIT**	
									Key Ideas and Details
●	●	●	●	●	●	●	●		**2.1** Ask and answer such questions as *who*, *what*, *where*, *when*, *why*, and *how* to demonstrate understanding of key details in a text.
●	●	●	●	●	●	●	●		**2.2** Identify the main topic of a multiparagraph text as well as the focus of specific paragraphs within the text.
●	●	●	●	●	●	●	●		**2.3** Describe the connection between a series of historical events, scientific ideas or concepts, or steps in technical procedures in a text.
									Craft and Structure
●	●	●	●	●	●	●	●		**2.4** Determine the meaning of words and phrases in a text relevant to a grade 2 topic or subject area.
●	●		●	●	●	●	●		**2.5** Know and use various text features (e.g., captions, bold print, subheadings, glossaries, indexes, electronic menus, icons) to locate key facts or information in a text efficiently.
●	●	●	●	●	●	●	●		**2.6** Identify the main purpose of a text, including what the author wants to answer, explain, or describe.
									Integration of Knowledge and Ideas
●	●	●	●	●	●	●	●		**2.7** Explain how specific images (e.g., a diagram showing how a machine works) contribute to and clarify a text.
●	●	●	●	●	●	●	●		**2.8** Describe how reasons support specific points the author makes in a text.
									Range of Reading and Level of Text Complexity
●	●	●	●	●	●	●	●		**2.10** By the end of the year, read and comprehend informational texts, including history/social studies, science, and technical texts, in the grades 2–3 text complexity band proficiently, with scaffolding as needed at the high end of the range.

Correlations
Common Core State Standards

	Science Selections							
RL Reading Standards for Literature, Grade 2	Apple Tree Swing	Parts of an Apple	Jack's Wheels	Six Simple Machines	What Will a Magnet Attract?	Magnificent Magnets	Stone Soup	Mexican Wedding Cakes
Key Ideas and Details								
2.1 Ask and answer such questions as *who, what, where, when, why,* and *how* to demonstrate understanding of key details in a text.	●		●			●	●	●
2.2 Recount stories, including fables and folktales from diverse cultures, and determine their central message, lesson, or moral.	●		●			●	●	●
2.3 Describe how characters in a story respond to major events and challenges.			●					●
Craft and Structure								
2.6 Acknowledge differences in the points of view of characters, including by speaking in a different voice for each character when reading dialogue aloud.			●			●	●	●
Integration of Knowledge and Ideas								
2.7 Use information gained from the illustrations and words in print or digital text to demonstrate understanding of its characters, setting, or plot.	●		●			●	●	●
Range of Reading and Level of Text Complexity								
2.10 By the end of the year, read and comprehend literature, including stories and poetry, in the grades 2–3 text complexity band proficiently, with scaffolding as needed at the high end of the range.	●		●			●	●	●

W Writing Standards, Grade 2								
Text Types and Purposes								
2.1 Write opinion pieces in which they introduce the topic or book they are writing about, state an opinion, supply reasons that support the opinion, use linking words (e.g., *because* and *also*) to connect opinion and reasons, and provide a concluding statement or section.			●	●				
2.2 Write informative/explanatory texts in which they introduce a topic, use facts and definitions to develop points, and provide a concluding statement or section.		●			●	●		

6

Reading Paired Text • EMC 1372 • © Evan-Moor Corp.

Corrections
Common Core State Standards

| Social Studies Selections | | | | | | | | Reading Standards for Literature, Grade 2 |
Mount Rushmore	Colossal Crazy Horse	Chavez and the Grape Boycott	King and the Bus Boycott	Railroad Songs	Tracks Across America	Farm Art	Wall of Welcome	**RL**
								**Key Ideas and Details**
●	●	●	●	●	●			**2.1** Ask and answer such questions as *who, what, where, when, why,* and *how* to demonstrate understanding of key details in a text.
								2.2 Recount stories, including fables and folktales from diverse cultures, and determine their central message, lesson, or moral.
		●	●					**2.3** Describe how characters in a story respond to major events and challenges.
								Craft and Structure
				●	●			**2.6** Acknowledge differences in the points of view of characters, including by speaking in a different voice for each character when reading dialogue aloud.
								Integration of Knowledge and Ideas
●	●	●	●	●	●			**2.7** Use information gained from the illustrations and words in print or digital text to demonstrate understanding of its characters, setting, or plot.
								Range of Reading and Level of Text Complexity
●	●	●	●	●	●			**2.10** By the end of the year, read and comprehend literature, including stories and poetry, in the grades 2–3 text complexity band proficiently, with scaffolding as needed at the high end of the range.

								W Writing Standards, Grade 2
								Text Types and Purposes
●	●				●			**2.1** Write opinion pieces in which they introduce the topic or book they are writing about, state an opinion, supply reasons that support the opinion, use linking words (e.g., *because* and *also*) to connect opinion and reasons, and provide a concluding statement or section.
		●	●	●	●	●	●	**2.2** Write informative/explanatory texts in which they introduce a topic, use facts and definitions to develop points, and provide a concluding statement or section.

Correlations
Texas Essential Knowledge and Skills

110.13. English Language Arts and Reading, Grade 2	Science Selections					
	Apple Tree Swing	Parts of an Apple	Jack's Wheels	Six Simple Machines	What Will a Magnet Attract?	Magnificent Magnets
Reading						
(5B) Vocabulary Development. Students understand new vocabulary and use it when reading and writing. Students are expected to use context to determine the relevant meaning of unfamiliar words or multiple-meaning words.	●	●	●	●	●	●
(9B) Comprehension of Literary Text/Fiction. Students understand, make inferences, and draw conclusions about the structure and elements of fiction and provide evidence from text to support their understanding. Students are expected to describe main characters in works of fiction, including their traits, motivations, and feelings.	●		●			●
(14A, B, C) Comprehension of Informational Text/Expository Text. Students analyze, make inferences and draw conclusions about and understand expository text and provide evidence from text to support their understanding. Students are expected to identify the main idea in a text and distinguish it from the topic; locate the facts that are clearly stated in a text; describe the order of events or ideas in a text.		●		●	●	
(14D) Comprehension of Informational Text/Expository Text. Students analyze, make inferences and draw conclusions about and understand expository text and provide evidence from text to support their understanding. Students are expected to use text features (e.g., table of contents, index, headings) to locate specific information in text.		●		●	●	
Writing						
(17A) Writing Process. Students use elements of the writing process (planning, drafting, revising, editing, publishing) to compose text. Students are expected to plan a first draft by generating ideas for writing (e.g., drawing, sharing ideas, listing key ideas).	●	●	●	●	●	●
(19A, C) Expository/Procedural Texts. Students write expository and procedural or work-related texts to communicate ideas and information to specific audiences for specific purposes. Students are expected to write brief compositions about topics of interest to the student; write brief comments on literary or informational texts.	●	●	●	●	●	●
(20) Persuasive Texts. Students write persuasive texts to influence the attitudes or actions of a specific audience on specific issues. Students are expected to write persuasive statements about issues that are important to the student for the appropriate audience in the school, home, or local community.			●	●		

Correlations
Texas Essential Knowledge and Skills

	Social Studies Selections								
Stone Soup	Mexican Wedding Cakes	Mount Rushmore	Colossal Crazy Horse	Chavez and the Grape Boycott	King and the Bus Boycott	Railroad Songs	Tracks Across America	Farm Art	Wall of Welcome
•	•	•	•	•	•	•	•	•	•
•	•								
		•	•	•	•	•	•	•	•
		•	•		•	•	•	•	•
•	•	•	•	•	•	•	•	•	•
•	•	•	•	•	•	•	•	•	•
		•	•						

How to Use

Reading Paired Text contains reading selections about grade-level science and social studies topics. The supporting comprehension and writing activities use Common Core methodology to guide students to closely examine the texts, discuss the topic, and ultimately improve their reading comprehension. The pairing of texts allows students to compare multiple viewpoints and provides opportunities to integrate information.

Each unit contains two thematically related selections that are focused around a Big Question. Each selection's activities include vocabulary development in context, an oral close reading discussion, comprehension questions, and a writing prompt. The unit assessment includes discussion of the topic, texts, and Big Question, as well as a writing prompt.

Unit Overview

The unit title, the topic-related student objective, and the Big Question are presented.

TOPIC INTRODUCTION
Background information connects students to the topic without giving away the selection content.

PAIRED TEXT SELECTIONS
Under each selection, genre and Guided Reading Levels (H–M) are listed, as well as teacher pages and student activities.

ASSESSMENT MATERIALS
At the end of the unit are activities that help students compare and integrate what they have learned about the topic.

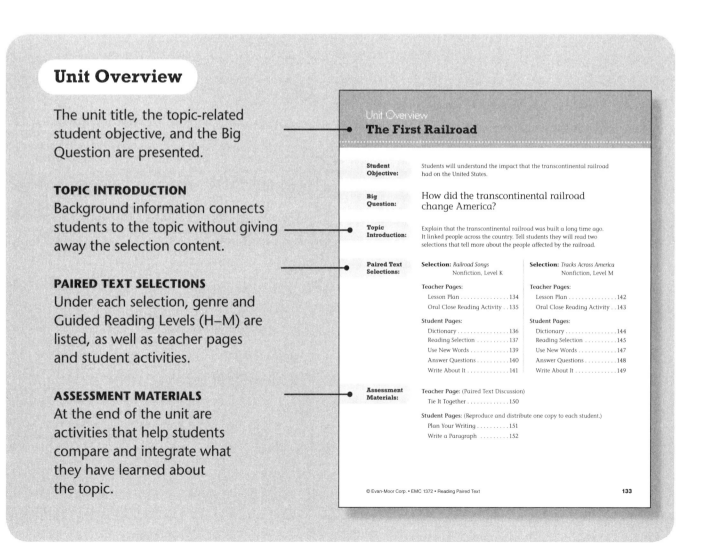

Unit Overview
The First Railroad

Student Objective:	Students will understand the impact that the transcontinental railroad had on the United States.
Big Question:	How did the transcontinental railroad change America?
Topic Introduction:	Explain that the transcontinental railroad was built a long time ago. It linked people across the country. Tell students they will read two selections that tell more about the people affected by the railroad.

Paired Text Selections:

Selection: *Railroad Songs*
Nonfiction, Level K

Teacher Pages:

Student Pages:

Selection: *Tracks Across America*
Nonfiction, Level M

Teacher Pages:

Student Pages:

Assessment Materials:

Teacher Page: (Paired Text Discussion)

Student Pages: (Reproduce and distribute one copy to each student.)

© Evan-Moor Corp. • EMC 1372 • Reading Paired Text   **133**

Teacher Pages

LESSON PLAN

The suggested teaching path guides you through each selection and related activities. It also provides selection-related background information for students to access before reading.

ORAL CLOSE READING ACTIVITY

These classroom discussion questions focus on important details and help students use context clues and word analysis to figure out the meaning of unfamiliar words.

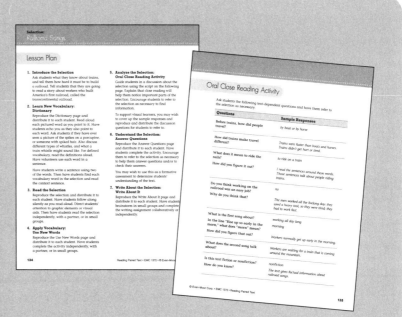

Student Pages

DICTIONARY

Academic vocabulary words from the selection are defined and lines are provided for students to write a sentence using two of the words.

SELECTIONS

Students read two selections on the unit topic. The topics should be familiar to students from their science and social studies lessons. Selections focus on a specific aspect of the topic and may offer multiple viewpoints. The texts are often augmented with illustrations, photos, diagrams, other graphics, and additional vocabulary support.

USE NEW WORDS

Students practice using new words by completing sentences with the appropriate vocabulary word.

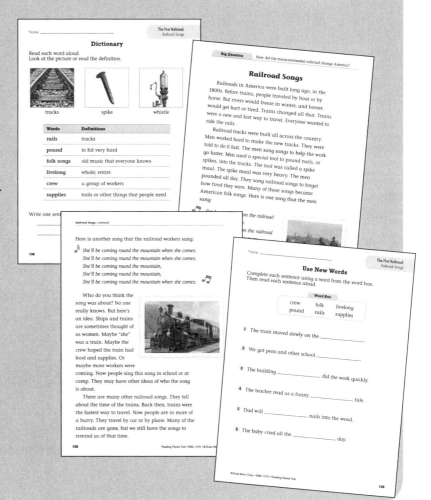

Student Pages, continued

ANSWER QUESTIONS
Students review key ideas of the selection by answering both literal and inferential questions.

WRITE ABOUT IT
Students further show what they have learned by writing. They arrange ideas and details in a graphic organizer, then respond to a text-based writing prompt.

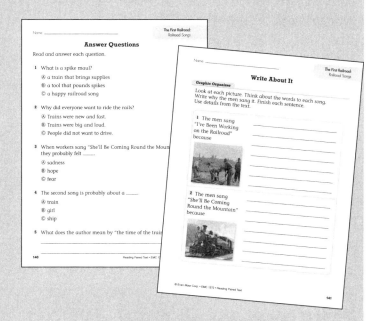

Assessment Materials

Teacher Page

TIE IT TOGETHER
Oral discussion questions tie together how both selections relate to the unit topic and the Big Question.

Student Pages

PLAN YOUR WRITING, WRITE A PARAGRAPH
Students arrange ideas and details from both selections in a graphic organizer, then respond to a topic-based writing prompt.

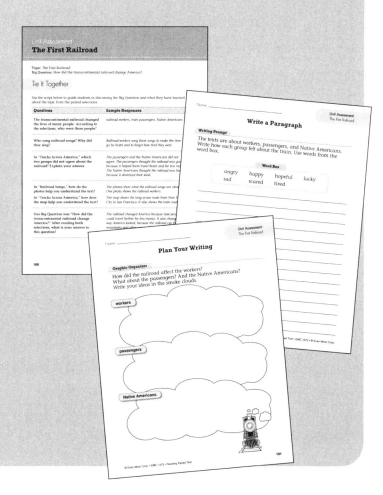

Parts of a Plant

Student Objective: Students will understand that plants have different parts that help them grow.

Big Question:

How do the parts of a plant help it grow?

Topic Introduction: Explain that trees and apples have different parts that help them grow. Tell students they will read two selections that tell more about the parts of an apple tree.

Paired Text Selections:

Assessment Materials:

Lesson Plan

1. Introduce the Selection

Show students an image of a tree. Ask them what they know about the different parts of a tree, and how those parts help the tree grow. Tell students that they are going to read a story about a girl and an apple tree.

2. Learn New Vocabulary: Dictionary

Reproduce the Dictionary page and distribute it to each student. Read aloud each pictured word as you point to it. Have students echo you as they also point to each word. Ask students to say how the roots of a tree are like drinking straws. Also discuss which parts of the tree are rough and which are smooth. For defined vocabulary, read the definitions aloud. Have volunteers use each word in a sentence.

Have students write a sentence using two of the words. Then have students find each vocabulary word in the selection and read the context sentence.

3. Read the Selection

Reproduce the selection and distribute it to each student. Have students follow along silently as you read aloud. Direct students' attention to graphic elements or visual aids. Then have students read the selection independently, with a partner, or in small groups.

4. Apply Vocabulary: Use New Words

Reproduce the Use New Words page and distribute it to each student. Have students complete the activity independently, with a partner, or in small groups.

5. Analyze the Selection: Oral Close Reading Activity

Guide students in a discussion about the selection using the script on the following page. Explain that close reading will help them notice important parts of the selection. Encourage students to refer to the selection as necessary to find information.

To support visual learners, you may wish to cover up the sample responses and reproduce and distribute the discussion questions for students to refer to.

6. Understand the Selection: Answer Questions

Reproduce the Answer Questions page and distribute it to each student. Have students complete the activity. Encourage them to refer to the selection as necessary to help them answer questions and/or to check their answers.

You may wish to use this as a formative assessment to determine students' understanding of the text.

7. Write About the Selection: Write About It

Reproduce the Write About It page and distribute it to each student. Have students brainstorm in small groups and complete the writing assignment collaboratively or independently.

Oral Close Reading Activity

Ask students the following text-dependent questions and have them refer to the selection as necessary.

Questions	Sample Responses
How does the trunk help the tree?	*It helps it stand strong and tall.*
What things does the tree branch hold?	*apples and a swing*
How does the girl know when to pick an apple?	*If the stem lets go of the branch, the apple is ripe.*
Think about picking apples. What should you do if the apple stem hangs on to the branch?	*Let the apple grow some more. It is not ripe yet.*
As the girl is swinging, she looks up. What does she see?	*the sun shining on the leaves*
What does it mean when leaves are green?	*They are making food for the tree.*
Why does the girl say the roots are thirsty?	*They take water up to the tree.*
What parts of a tree are mentioned in the story?	*trunk, bark, branch, apples, leaves, roots*

Dictionary

Read each word aloud.
Look at the picture or read the definition.

trunk

roots

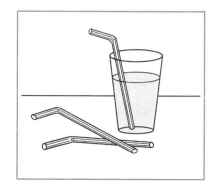

straws

Words	Definitions
harvest	to pick fruits and vegetables from the garden
rough	not smooth
bark	the outer part of a tree trunk
branch	the part of the tree that grows out
ripe	ready to eat

Write one sentence using two of the words.

_____

_____

Apple Tree Swing

I like visiting my grandparents in the fall. This is when we harvest the apples from their tree. This apple tree has been around since my mom was a girl. It's a great old apple tree. Its thick trunk helps it stand strong and tall. The rough bark protects the tree from insects and other things.

A swing hangs from a strong branch of the tree. It is my swing. As you know, branches don't just hold swings. Branches hold apples, and these apples are the best! Some of the apples are ripe now. I know they are ripe because the skin is rosy. The flesh is crispy and sweet.

I cup an apple in my hand and gently push it upward. If it comes off the branch easily, it's ready. If the stem hangs on, it means the apple has more growing to do. Today we picked enough apples for two pies!

Grandma's pies are yummy. We had warm apple pie with vanilla ice cream. Grandpa told stories of when Mom was little, swinging on her apple tree swing. Now it's my turn. I like to swing slowly. As I swing, I look up. The sun shines on the leaves, making them bright green. Grandma says that when the leaves are green like that, they are making food. They make food with sunlight, air, and water. The water comes up from the tree's roots. The roots are below the ground. I imagine the roots are like straws, taking water up to the tree.

I love the apple tree, with its wide trunk and strong branches. I love its thirsty roots and green leaves. I love its rough bark and skinny stems. But most of all, I love its sweet apples and old swing.

Name: _____

Use New Words

Complete each sentence using a word from the word box.
Then read each sentence aloud.

Word Box

bark	branch	harvest
ripe	roots	rough

1 The sandpaper felt very _____.

2 The _____ of the tree is like a coat.

3 There were too many apples on the _____,
and it broke off.

4 We watered the tree near the _____.

5 The farmer needs help gathering his _____.

6 Peaches are soft and fuzzy when they are _____.

Answer Questions

Read and answer each question.

1 How does a branch help a tree?

   Ⓐ It makes food for the tree.

   Ⓑ It holds the swing.

   Ⓒ It holds the apples.

2 Which words help you understand what the roots do?

   Ⓐ They make food with sunlight, air, and water.

   Ⓑ The roots are like straws.

   Ⓒ The roots are below the ground.

3 Which part of the tree does the girl like the most?

   Ⓐ fruit

   Ⓑ trunk

   Ⓒ leaves

4 How does the bark protect the tree?

_____

_____

5 How do you know that an apple is ready to pick?

_____

_____

Name: _____

Write About It

Graphic Organizer

Label the parts of an apple tree.
Then write how each part helps the tree.

Lesson Plan

1. Introduce the Selection

Show students an image of an apple. Ask them what they know about the different parts of an apple, and how those parts help the apple grow. Tell students that they are going to read a nonfiction selection about the parts of an apple.

2. Learn New Vocabulary: Dictionary

Reproduce the Dictionary page and distribute it to each student. Read aloud each pictured word as you point to it. Have students echo you as they also point to each word. Have students point out the similarities between the pockets in their clothing and a seed pocket. Also have them compare an apple's skin to their own skin. For defined vocabulary, read the definitions aloud. Have volunteers use each word in a sentence.

Have students write a sentence using two of the words. Then have students find each vocabulary word in the selection and read the context sentence.

3. Read the Selection

Reproduce the selection and distribute it to each student. Have students follow along silently as you read aloud. Direct students' attention to graphic elements or visual aids. Then have students read the selection independently, with a partner, or in small groups.

4. Apply Vocabulary: Use New Words

Reproduce the Use New Words page and distribute it to each student. Have students complete the activity independently, with a partner, or in small groups.

5. Analyze the Selection: Oral Close Reading Activity

Guide students in a discussion about the selection using the script on the following page. Explain that close reading will help them notice important parts of the selection. Encourage students to refer to the selection as necessary to find information.

To support visual learners, you may wish to cover up the sample responses and reproduce and distribute the discussion questions for students to refer to.

6. Understand the Selection: Answer Questions

Reproduce the Answer Questions page and distribute it to each student. Have students complete the activity. Encourage them to refer to the selection as necessary to help them answer questions and/or to check their answers.

You may wish to use this as a formative assessment to determine students' understanding of the text.

7. Write About the Selection: Write About It

Reproduce the Write About It page and distribute it to each student. Have students brainstorm in small groups and complete the writing assignment collaboratively or independently.

Oral Close Reading Activity

Ask students the following text-dependent questions and have them refer to the selection as necessary.

Questions	Sample Responses
What are the six main parts of an apple?	*stem, leaf, core, skin, flesh, seed*
What parts of the apple are normally eaten?	*skin and flesh*
What is the stem's job?	*It turns the leaf toward the sunlight.* *It holds the apple to the tree.*
The author talks about the "insides" of an apple. What are the names of these parts?	*core, flesh, seed*
What are the "outside" parts?	*stem, leaf, skin*
Why does the author say that a seed is a new apple tree waiting to happen?	*Apple trees grow from seeds.*
How does the seed pocket help the apple grow?	*It contains the seeds of the apple.*
How do the pictures help you understand the text?	*We can see the parts of the apple labeled.* *We can see the star-shaped seed pocket.*

Name: _____

Dictionary

Read each word aloud.
Look at the picture or read the definition.

leaf

core

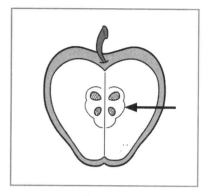

seed pocket

Words	Definitions
nutritious	good for you
stem	the tiny twig that holds the fruit to the tree
skin	the part that covers the outside and protects the inside
flesh	the juicy part of the fruit that you eat
seed	this holds the material needed to grow a new plant

Write one sentence using two of the words.

_____

_____

Parts of an Apple

Nutritious and juicy, an apple is a sweet treat. An apple has six parts, each with a job to do.

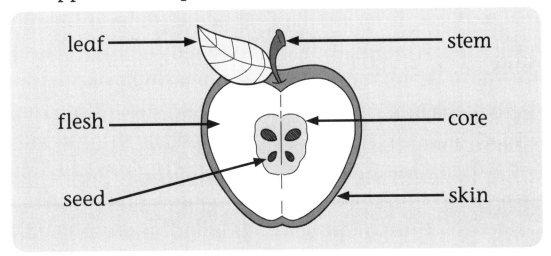

Stem The stem is at the top of the apple. It looks like a tiny twig. The stem has leaves growing from it. It helps the leaves face the sun so they can make food. The stem also holds the apple to the tree.

Leaf An apple leaf is smooth and green on the top. It is fuzzy and silver-green on the bottom. The leaf uses water, sunlight, and air to make food for the tree. Water and air come and go through tiny holes in the leaf. The veins carry water and food to the rest of the tree.

Core The core is at the center of the apple. Its main job is to keep the seeds. Most people do not eat the core, since it has hard seeds.

Skin The skin is smooth and sometimes waxy. It can be green, red, pink, yellow, or a mix of these colors. The skin protects the insides of the apple and keeps it juicy. Did you know that the skin is the most nutritious part of the apple? If you want lots of vitamins, eat the skin!

Flesh The flesh is the best part of the apple. It tastes good! The color of the flesh can be anywhere from snow white to bright red. The flesh is full of water. That is why it is so juicy. This is the part that goes into pie, juice, and applesauce.

Seed A seed is a new apple tree waiting to happen. If you slice an apple across, you will have a circle. See the star in the center? That's the seed pocket. All apples have five seed pockets. The number of seeds in each seed pocket depends on the kind of apple.

Some apple parts are good to eat and some are not. But all six apple parts work together to help the apple grow. They help the apple get big and juicy. Then you can eat it!

Use New Words

Complete each sentence using a word from the word box.
Then read each sentence aloud.

Word Box

flesh	leaf	nutritious
seed	skin	stem

1 The _____ of a plum is firm and purple.

2 Protect your _____ so you don't get sunburned.

3 We need to eat _____ food to stay healthy.

4 I planted a _____ and now I have a little plant.

5 The pink rose has a long _____ with thorns.

6 In the fall, every _____ falls off the tree.

Answer Questions

Read and answer each question.

1 Which of these makes food for the tree?

Ⓐ flesh

Ⓑ skin

Ⓒ leaf

2 Which word tells about the word **core**?

Ⓐ outside

Ⓑ center

Ⓒ bottom

3 Which word tells about the job of the apple skin?

Ⓐ protect

Ⓑ feed

Ⓒ attach

4 How are a twig and a stem similar?

_____

_____

5 What does the author want you to know about the parts of an apple?

_____

_____

Name: _____

Write About It

Write the names of the apple parts.
Write how each part helps the apple grow.

What is your favorite way to eat an apple? Write a paragraph
about it. Use details from the selections.

_____

_____

_____

_____

Parts of a Plant

Topic: Parts of a Plant

Big Question: How do the parts of a plant help it grow?

Tie It Together

Use the script below to guide students in discussing the Big Question and what they have learned about the topic from the paired selections.

Questions	Sample Responses
What words are used in the selections to describe the flesh of an apple?	*crispy, sweet, juicy, best, good, snow white, bright red*
What words from both selections tell about the skin of an apple?	*rosy, smooth, waxy, green, red, pink, yellow, nutritious*
According to "Apple Tree Swing," what are the parts of a tree?	*The parts of a tree are the trunk, bark, branches, apples, leaves, and roots.*
According to "Parts of an Apple," what are the parts of an apple?	*The parts of an apple are the stem, leaf, core, skin, flesh, and seed.*
What part of the tree protects the insides of the tree from insects?	*the bark*
What part of the apple protects the insides of the apple?	*the skin*
Our Big Question was "How do the parts of a plant help it grow?" How did "Apple Tree Swing" answer this question?	*The story "Apple Tree Swing" talked about the parts of a tree, which is a plant. The trunk keeps the tree tall. The bark protects the tree from insects. The branches hold apples. The leaves make food for the tree. The roots take water up to the tree.*
How did "Parts of an Apple" answer it?	*The selection "Parts of an Apple" talked about the parts of an apple, which is a part of a plant. The parts of the apple help it grow, too. The stem holds the apple to the tree. The skin protects the insides. The leaf makes food for the tree. The core holds the seeds, and the seeds help make more trees.*

Plan Your Writing

Think about what you have learned about apples.
Write words that tell how an apple looks, feels, sounds,
smells, and tastes.

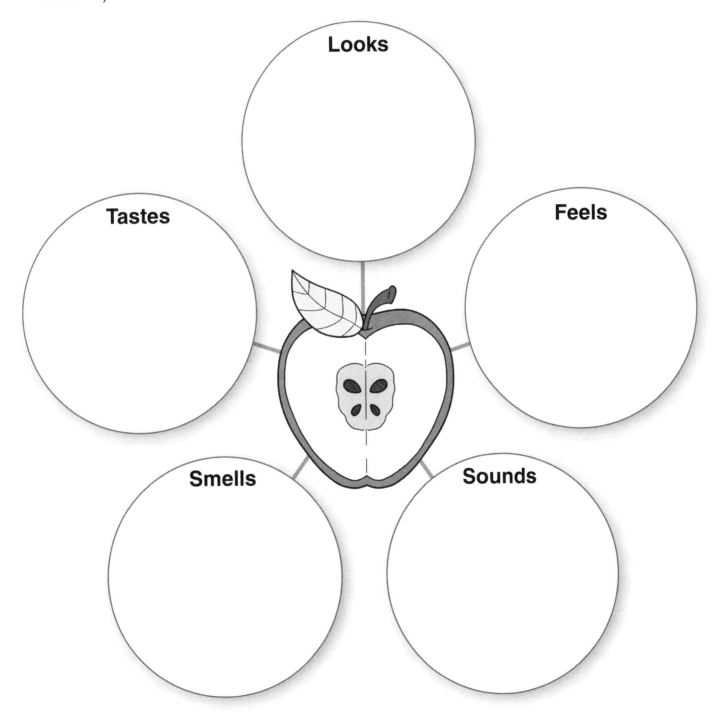

Looks

Tastes

Feels

Smells

Sounds

Write a Paragraph

Writing Prompt

Use the words in the box to describe the parts of an apple.
Write how each part helps the apple grow.

Word Box

fuzzy	green	juicy	nutritious
red	smooth	sweet	waxy

The fuzzy green leaf helps the apple get food.

_____

_____

_____

_____

_____

_____

_____

_____

_____

_____

_____

Simple Machines Help Us

Student Objective: Students will recognize six simple machines they use in everyday life.

Big Question:
How do simple machines help us?

Topic Introduction: Explain that simple machines are tools that have few or no moving parts. Tell students they will read two selections that tell more about simple machines.

Paired Text Selections:

Assessment Materials:

Lesson Plan

1. **Introduce the Selection**

   Help students name some simple machines. Then tell students that they are going to read a story about a boy who uses a simple machine to make his work easier. Read the title aloud and ask students to predict what the simple machine could be. (wheels and axle)

2. **Learn New Vocabulary: Dictionary**

   Reproduce the Dictionary page and distribute it to each student. Read aloud each pictured word as you point to it. Have students echo you as they also point to each word. Ask students if they have ever ridden a skateboard. Ask them what makes the skateboard move. (wheels and axle) Have them point to the wheels in the pictures. Have students point to their knees and elbows. For defined vocabulary, read the definitions aloud. Have volunteers use each word in a sentence.

   Have volunteers say a sentence using two of the words. Then have students find each vocabulary word in the selection and read the context sentence.

3. **Read the Selection**

   Reproduce the selection and distribute it to each student. Have students follow along silently as you read aloud. Direct students' attention to graphic elements or visual aids. Then have students read the selection independently, with a partner, or in small groups.

4. **Apply Vocabulary: Use New Words**

   Reproduce the Use New Words page and distribute it to each student. Have students complete the activity independently, with a partner, or in small groups.

5. **Analyze the Selection: Oral Close Reading Activity**

   Guide students in a discussion about the selection using the script on the following page. Explain that close reading will help them notice important parts of the selection. Encourage students to refer to the selection as necessary to find information.

   To support visual learners, you may wish to cover up the sample responses and reproduce and distribute the discussion questions for students to refer to.

6. **Understand the Selection: Answer Questions**

   Reproduce the Answer Questions page and distribute it to each student. Have students complete the activity. Encourage them to refer to the selection as necessary to help them answer questions and/or to check their answers.

   You may wish to use this as a formative assessment to determine students' understanding of the text.

7. **Write About the Selection: Write About It**

   Reproduce the Write About It page and distribute it to each student. Have students brainstorm in small groups and complete the writing assignment collaboratively or independently.

Oral Close Reading Activity

Ask students the following text-dependent questions and have them refer to the selection as necessary.

Questions	Sample Responses
Jack's dad travels in a car, and Jack travels on his skateboard. How are the car and the skateboard similar?	*They both have wheels. They both help people move.*
How does Jack get to Andrew's house?	*on his skateboard*
Why does Dad want to look at Jack's skateboard?	*It is wobbly. He needs to fix the wheels.*
Does Jack listen to his dad when he offers to take a look at the wheels?	*no*
Why not?	*Jack wants to go to his friend's house first.*
What time must Jack be home?	*6:00*
What time does he leave Andrew's house?	*5:55*
If Jack left at 5:55, and he needs to be home by 6:00, how much time is he giving himself?	*5 minutes*
How long does it actually take Jack to get home this time?	*20 minutes*
Why did it take so long?	*Jack walked home because he couldn't use his skateboard. His skateboard would have made him travel faster.*
If Dad had fixed the skateboard, do you think Jack would have gotten home on time?	*yes*
Why do you think that?	*The skateboard would have helped him go fast. He would have gotten home on time.*
Is this selection fiction or nonfiction?	*fiction*
How do you know?	*The selection tells a story, it has a main character, and it gives the reader a message.*

Dictionary

Read each word aloud.
Look at the picture or read the definition.

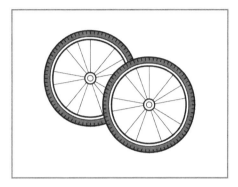

wheels

skateboard

knee

elbow

Words	Definitions
wobbly	shaky or unsteady
opposite	on the other side
agreement	thinking the same way
tumbled	fell in a clumsy way
useless	of no use; broken
limped	walked in a funny way because it hurts

Jack's Wheels

Jack rolled into the driveway on his skateboard as Dad was getting home from work. Dad stepped out of the car and Jack greeted him: "Hey, Dad!"

"Hi, son. Your skateboard is wobbly. You shouldn't be riding it. Let me look at the wheels."

"Not now, Dad," answered Jack. "I'm going to Andrew's house. He has a new video game. See you later!" Off he rolled on his wobbly skateboard. Jack and Andrew lived at opposite ends of the block, but on his skateboard, Jack could quickly zoom down the sidewalk.

"Be home by six!" shouted Dad after Jack, and Jack waved in agreement.

The boys played video games for a while, and then Jack looked at the clock. It was 5:55. He would have just enough time to skate home.

"I need to go," said Jack, heading for the door.

"Okay, see you later," answered Andrew.

Jack hopped onto his skateboard and started rolling down the street. Suddenly…*wobble, wobble, bump!* Jack tumbled to the ground. Ouch! His knee and elbow were banged up pretty badly, and so was his skateboard. The wheel had cracked! With his bloody knee and useless skateboard, Jack limped all the way home.

Jack finally got home at 6:15. By this time, his knee was really hurting. To make things worse, his dad was frowning at the broken wheel. Jack knew what was coming.

"I know," said Jack. "I should have listened to you."

Use New Words

Complete each sentence using a word from the word box.
Then read each sentence aloud.

Word Box

agreement	limped	opposite
tumbled	useless	wobbly

1 The clothes _____ around in the dryer.

2 The pen was _____ without ink.

3 The baby deer was still _____ on its feet.

4 When I hurt my ankle, I _____ for three days.

5 Antonyms are words that mean the _____.

6 They were in _____, so they shook hands.

Name: _____

Answer Questions

Read and answer each question.

1 Why is Jack's skateboard wobbly?

    Ⓐ It is missing one wheel.

    Ⓑ Something is wrong with the wheel.

    Ⓒ Jack banged the board on the ground.

2 Which word best tells how Jack's skateboard moves?

    Ⓐ walk

    Ⓑ roll

    Ⓒ ride

3 Why does Jack get hurt?

    Ⓐ Jack was going too fast.

    Ⓑ Dad did not fix the wheel.

    Ⓒ Jack was doing a big jump.

4 How do you think Dad feels when he sees Jack at 6:15?

    Ⓐ He is worried about Jack.

    Ⓑ He is happy to see Jack.

    Ⓒ He is busy with something else.

5 What do you think will happen next?

_____

_____

Name: _____

Write About It

Think about what happened to Jack and how he changes from the beginning of the story to the end. Write about it. Include details from the story.

How Jack felt at the beginning and why	
What happened to Jack and how he felt when it happened	
What happened after Jack got home	

Lesson Plan

1. Introduce the Selection

Point out things that use simple machines that students use often, such as a bike, window blinds, scissors, or a stapler. Ask students to think about how they would manage without these items. All these things use simple machines, and they make work easier. Tell students that they are going to read a nonfiction selection about six simple machines.

2. Learn New Vocabulary: Dictionary

Reproduce the Dictionary page and distribute it to each student. Read aloud each pictured word as you point to it. Have students echo you as they also point to each word. Ask students if they have ever used a hammer. Explain that when a hammer is used to pull out a nail, the hammer is a lever. Have students make a wedge shape with their arms. For defined vocabulary, read the definitions aloud. Have volunteers use each word in a sentence.

Have students write a sentence using two of the words. Then have students find each vocabulary word in the selection and read the context sentence.

3. Read the Selection

Reproduce the selection and distribute it to each student. Have students follow along silently as you read aloud. Direct students' attention to graphic elements or visual aids. Then have students read the selection independently, with a partner, or in small groups.

4. Apply Vocabulary: Use New Words

Reproduce the Use New Words page and distribute it to each student. Have students complete the activity independently, with a partner, or in small groups.

5. Analyze the Selection: Oral Close Reading Activity

Guide students in a discussion about the selection using the script on the following page. Explain that close reading will help them notice important parts of the selection. Encourage students to refer to the selection as necessary to find information.

To support visual learners, you may wish to cover up the sample responses and reproduce and distribute the discussion questions for students to refer to.

6. Understand the Selection: Answer Questions

Reproduce the Answer Questions page and distribute it to each student. Have students complete the activity. Encourage them to refer to the selection as necessary to help them answer questions and/or to check their answers.

You may wish to use this as a formative assessment to determine students' understanding of the text.

7. Write About the Selection: Write About It

Reproduce the Write About It page and distribute it to each student. Have students brainstorm in small groups and complete the writing assignment collaboratively or independently.

Oral Close Reading Activity

Ask students the following text-dependent questions and have them refer to the selection as necessary.

Questions	Sample Responses
How does a lever make work easier?	*A lever helps us to raise or move something.*
Name an example of a lever.	*hammer*
How do a wheel and axle make work easier?	*They help to move things across the ground.*
What are two things that move with a wheel and axle?	*car and skateboard*
Think about the wheel and axle and the wheel on a pulley. How does the wheel on a pulley look different from the wheel on an axle?	*The wheel on the pulley has raised edges so that a rope can stay on the wheel.*
How are a wheel and axle similar to a pulley?	*They both move things.*
How are they different?	*The wheel and axle move things along the ground. The pulley moves things up, down, and across.*
How might an inclined plane make work easier?	*You can pull something up a ramp instead of up stairs.*
How does a rotating stool work?	*It has a screw that helps it move up and down.*
Besides making things go up and down, what else does a screw do?	*It holds things together.*
Why is a wedge a type of inclined plane?	*It has one end that is wider than the other.*
Look at the pictures of the ramp and the wedge. What does a wedge do that a ramp does not do?	*A wedge cuts, pierces, or splits things.*
How do the pictures help you understand the text?	*We can see examples of the simple machines and what they can do.*

Name: _____

Dictionary

Read each word aloud.
Look at the picture or read the definition.

hammer

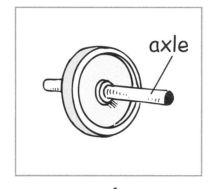

axle

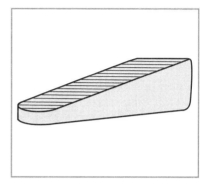

wedge

Words	Definitions
simple	easy to understand or easy to do
effort	physical energy; work
load	something carried or moved
inclined	slanted
rotating	turning
pierces	pokes with a sharp pointy object

Write one sentence using two of the words.

_____

_____

Six Simple Machines

Simple machines help us by making work easier and faster. There are six types of simple machines. These machines are all around you.

Lever A lever is a board or bar. A lever raises or moves something with less effort. A lever has a turning point called a fulcrum. The object that the lever moves is called the load.

A hammer is a type of lever.

Wheel and Axle A wheel and axle help to move something across the ground. When the wheel turns, the axle turns, too. The axle is the bar attached to the center of the wheel.

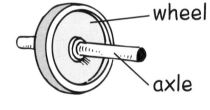

Cars, skateboards, and bikes move with wheels and axles.

Pulley A pulley moves objects up, down, and across. A pulley has a wheel with raised edges. The raised edges help a rope or chain stay on the wheel.

When you pull down on the pulley, the blinds go up.

Inclined Plane Things move up and down an inclined plane. An inclined plane is a flat surface. One end is raised higher than the other.

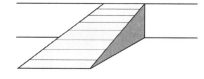

A ramp is an inclined plane.

Screw A screw is a type of inclined plane that curves around a pole. A screw raises and lowers things. Screws also hold things together.

This rotating stool has a screw that moves the seat up and down.

The screw on this light bulb holds the bulb to the socket.

Wedge A wedge is also a type of inclined plane. It is wide on one end and pointy at the other end. A wedge cuts, pierces, or splits things.

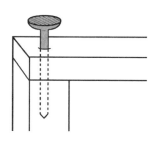

A nail is a wedge. It pierces the wood.

Simple machines make our lives easier. Without them, some jobs would be impossible to do. Try moving a car without wheels or splitting wood without an ax!

A wedge splits the wood open.

Name: _____

Use New Words

Complete each sentence using a word from the word box.
Then read each sentence aloud.

Word Box

effort	inclined	load
pierces	rotating	simple

1 I carried a _____ of books from school.

2 The ramp was a little _____, so it was easy to use.

3 The addition problem was _____, so I knew the answer.

4 The sharp needle _____ the fabric.

5 The blades on the fan were _____ slowly.

6 It takes a lot of _____ to run a race.

Answer Questions

Read and answer each question.

1 Which of these is a kind of lever?

   Ⓐ light bulb

   Ⓑ hammer

   Ⓒ wedge

2 Which words tell you what **inclined** means?

   Ⓐ flat surface at one end

   Ⓑ one end raised higher than the other

   Ⓒ easy to move things

3 Blinds are raised and lowered using a _____.

   Ⓐ lever

   Ⓑ pulley

   Ⓒ screw

4 Which simple machine is used for splitting or cutting?

   Ⓐ wedge

   Ⓑ pulley

   Ⓒ wheel and axle

5 A lever lifts things. What does a screw do?

   _____

   _____

Name: _____

Write About It

Graphic Organizer

Look at the pictures.
Which simple machine would make the work easier?
Tell why.

Word Box

inclined plane	lever	pulley
screw	wedge	wheel and axle

Simple Machines Help Us

Topic: Simple Machines Help Us
Big Question: How do simple machines help us?

Tie It Together

Use the script below to guide students in discussing the Big Question and what they have learned about the topic from the paired selections.

Questions	Sample Responses
A skateboard has wheels and axles. What other simple machines with wheels and axles can you think of?	*car, bike, go-cart, truck, wheelbarrow, rolling chair, shopping cart*
In "Jack's Wheels," what is the load? Is it the wheels, the sidewalk, or Jack himself? Explain your answer.	*Jack, because a load is something that is carried or moved.*
In "Jack's Wheels," it says that "Jack rolled into the driveway on his skateboard." What detail from "Six Simple Machines" explains this idea?	*A wheel and axle help to move something across the ground.*
What type of simple machine is in both selections?	*wheel and axle*
Our Big Question was "How do simple machines help us?" How did "Six Simple Machines" answer this question?	*This selection told the names of the six simple machines and how they help us.*
How did "Jack's Wheels" answer it?	*"Jack's Wheels" told how the wheels and axles on the skateboard helped Jack travel easily to his friend's house. It also showed what happened when this simple machine broke and he couldn't use it.*

Plan Your Writing

Write words or draw pictures to help you remember each simple machine.

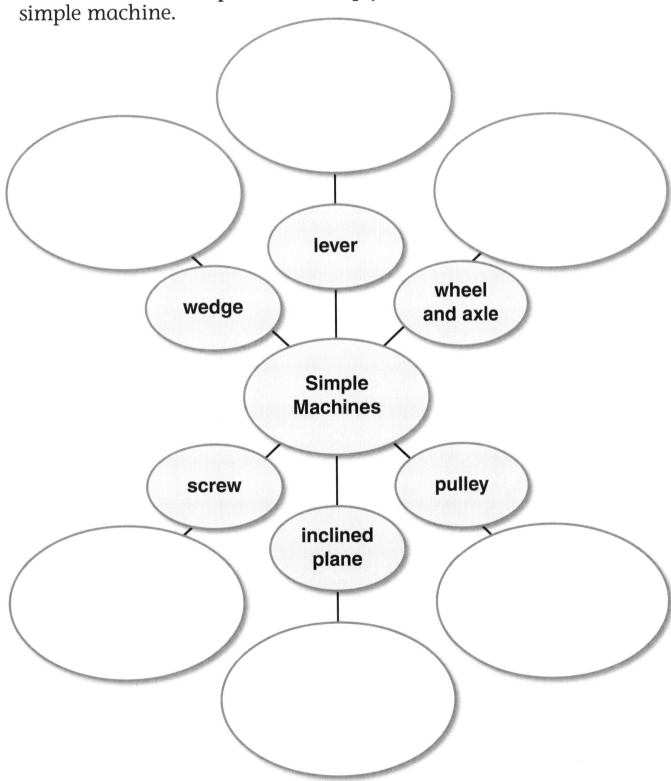

Write a Paragraph

Writing Prompt

In "Jack's Wheels," Jack was late because of a broken wheel.

• Which simple machine could have helped Jack get home in time?

• Use words from the word box. Use details from "Six Simple Machines."

Word Box

inclined plane	lever	pulley
screw	wedge	wheel and axle

_____

_____

_____

_____

_____

_____

_____

_____

_____

_____

_____

Understanding Magnets

Student Objective: Students will understand that a magnet will attract anything that contains iron.

Big Question:

Does a magnet stick to all shiny things?

Topic Introduction: Explain that magnetism is a force that is all around us. Tell students they will read two selections that tell more about the force of magnets.

Paired Text Selections:

Assessment Materials:

Lesson Plan

1. Introduce the Selection

Have small magnets available for students to use throughout the unit. Ask students to think about their refrigerator at home. Does it have any magnets on it? If it does, that's because the refrigerator is made of steel, and magnets attract steel. Tell students that they are going to read a nonfiction selection about the types of things that magnets attract.

2. Learn New Vocabulary: Dictionary

Reproduce the Dictionary page and distribute it to each student. Read aloud each pictured word as you point to it. Have students echo you as they also point to each word. For defined vocabulary, read the definitions aloud. Have volunteers use each word in a sentence. Focus on *magnets*, *magnetism*, and *magnetic*, calling attention to the underlined suffixes. Discuss the difference in meaning. Clap out the syllables in each word, clapping harder on the stressed syllables: *MAG-nets*, *MAG-net-ism*, *mag-NET-ic*. Help students notice how the stressed syllable changes in *magnetic*.

Have students write a sentence using two of the words. Then have students find each vocabulary word in the selection and read the context sentence.

3. Read the Selection

Reproduce the selection and distribute it to each student. Have students follow along silently as you read aloud. Direct students' attention to graphic elements or visual aids. Then have students read the selection independently, with a partner, or in small groups.

4. Apply Vocabulary: Use New Words

Reproduce the Use New Words page and distribute it to each student. Have students complete the activity independently, with a partner, or in small groups.

5. Analyze the Selection: Oral Close Reading Activity

Guide students in a discussion about the selection using the script on the following page. Explain that close reading will help them notice important parts of the selection. Encourage students to refer to the selection as necessary to find information.

To support visual learners, you may wish to cover up the sample responses and reproduce and distribute the discussion questions for students to refer to.

6. Understand the Selection: Answer Questions

Reproduce the Answer Questions page and distribute it to each student. Have students complete the activity. Encourage them to refer to the selection as necessary to help them answer questions and/or to check their answers.

You may wish to use this as a formative assessment to determine students' understanding of the text.

7. Write About the Selection: Write About It

Reproduce the Write About It page and distribute it to each student. Have students brainstorm in small groups and complete the writing assignment collaboratively or independently.

Oral Close Reading Activity

Ask students the following text-dependent questions and have them refer to the selection as necessary.

Questions	Sample Responses
How are the papers held up on the refrigerator?	*with magnets*
Would a window be attracted to a magnet?	*no*
How do you know?	*I read that a magnetic object will not attract things like glass or wood. A window is made of glass.*
Would a magnet stick to a penny or a dime?	*no*
Why do you think that?	*I read that a magnet will not stick to coins. Pennies and dimes are coins.*
Why would a magnet attract steel?	*Steel contains iron.*
What is one thing made of steel?	*refrigerator*
Why wouldn't a refrigerator magnet hold up a book?	*The book is not thin enough. The magnet is not strong enough.*
Is this text fiction or nonfiction?	*nonfiction*
How do you know?	*The text gives facts about what things will stick to magnets or not.*

Dictionary

Read each word aloud.
Look at the picture or read the definition.

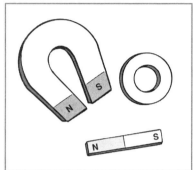

magnets

refrigerator

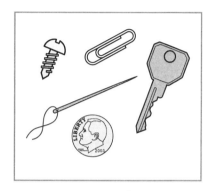

metals

Words	Definitions
attract	to pull together
force	power
magnetism	natural force between magnetic objects
magnetic	able to attract some metals; able to act like a magnet
coins	money made of flat metal

Write one sentence using two of the words.

_____

_____

Reading Paired Text • EMC 1372 • © Evan-Moor Corp.

What Will a Magnet Attract?

How do the papers on this refrigerator stick to the door? They aren't glued on. Magnets hold the papers there. Magnets also keep refrigerator doors shut.

Magnets come in many shapes and sizes. Here are just a few:

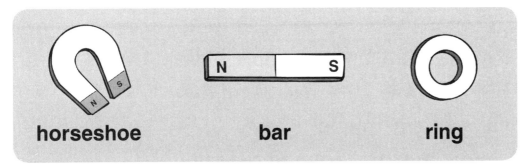

horseshoe   **bar**   **ring**

Magnets stick to objects made from some kinds of metals. Magnets use a force called magnetism to attract these metals. An object that attracts metal is called magnetic. A magnetic object will not attract things like glass or wood.

A magnet will not stick to all things made of metal. A magnet will not stick to coins. They do not have iron in them. Magnets only attract metals with iron in them. Steel is a metal with iron in it.

A magnet will attract some things made of steel. Many refrigerators are made of magnetic steel. So are things like paper clips, pins, nails, and cars.

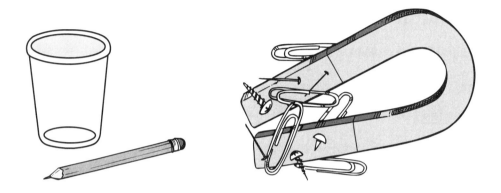

Most magnets will attract a metal object even if something thin is between the object and the magnet. Hang a picture on the refrigerator, and a magnet will hold it in place. But a refrigerator magnet won't hold up a book. The magnet isn't strong enough.

A refrigerator is just one magnetic object. Look around. Find something that a magnet might attract. It shouldn't be too hard to find. Magnetism is all around!

Use New Words

Complete each sentence using a word from the word box.
Then read each sentence aloud.

Word Box

attract	coins	force
magnetic	magnetism	

1 The magnet sticks to the _____ bookshelf.

2 We planted flowers to _____ butterflies.

3 The _____ added up to 45 cents.

4 I needed great _____ to open the window.

5 _____ is all around.

Answer Questions

Read and answer each question.

1 Magnets attract some objects made of _____.

Ⓐ glass

Ⓑ metal

Ⓒ cloth

2 Which of these would be attracted to a magnet?

Ⓐ pencil

Ⓑ paper clip

Ⓒ penny

3 A magnet attracts metal that contains _____.

Ⓐ sand

Ⓑ iron

Ⓒ coins

4 Why won't a magnet stick to a dime?

Ⓐ A dime doesn't have iron.

Ⓑ A dime doesn't have paper.

Ⓒ A dime doesn't have metal.

5 Why does the author say magnetism is all around?

_____

_____

Name: _____

Write About It

Graphic Organizer

What things will a magnet stick to?
Answer with words or drawings.
If you need help, look back at the text.

Writing Prompt

Finish the sentence.

A magnet will stick to _____

_____

_____

Lesson Plan

1. **Introduce the Selection**

   Help students identify different things made of metal, such as a stapler, a doorknob, and paper clips. Ask them to predict which ones a magnet will stick to. Then tell students that they are going to read a story about a girl who learns about magnetic and nonmagnetic metals.

2. **Learn New Vocabulary: Dictionary**

   Reproduce the Dictionary page and distribute it to each student. Read aloud each pictured word as you point to it. Have students echo you as they also point to each word. Clarify that many, but not all, electric can openers have a magnet that attracts the lid of the can. For defined vocabulary, read the definitions aloud. Have volunteers use each word in a sentence.

   Have students write a sentence using two of the words. Then have students find each vocabulary word in the selection and read the context sentence.

3. **Read the Selection**

   Reproduce the selection and distribute it to each student. Have students follow along silently as you read aloud. Direct students' attention to graphic elements or visual aids. Then have students read the selection independently, with a partner, or in small groups.

4. **Apply Vocabulary: Use New Words**

   Reproduce the Use New Words page and distribute it to each student. Have students complete the activity independently, with a partner, or in small groups.

5. **Analyze the Selection: Oral Close Reading Activity**

   Guide students in a discussion about the selection using the script on the following page. Explain that close reading will help them notice important parts of the selection. Encourage students to refer to the selection as necessary to find information.

   To support visual learners, you may wish to cover up the sample responses and reproduce and distribute the discussion questions for students to refer to.

6. **Understand the Selection: Answer Questions**

   Reproduce the Answer Questions page and distribute it to each student. Have students complete the activity. Encourage them to refer to the selection as necessary to help them answer questions and/or to check their answers.

   You may wish to use this as a formative assessment to determine students' understanding of the text.

7. **Write About the Selection: Write About It**

   Reproduce the Write About It page and distribute it to each student. Have students brainstorm in small groups and complete the writing assignment collaboratively or independently.

Oral Close Reading Activity

Ask students the following text-dependent questions and have them refer to the selection as necessary.

Questions	Sample Responses
What kind of refrigerator magnets do Lisa and Pete play with?	*word and letter magnets*
The can opener in the story has a magnet. What is the magnet used for?	*to hold the lid of the can*
What are some magnets in Lisa's kitchen?	*refrigerator magnets, can opener magnet, cabinet magnet*
Where is the magnet in Lisa's bathroom?	*in the shower curtain*
What is it used for?	*to help the curtain stick to the tub*
What is the main difference between the magnets at home and the magnet at Dad's work?	*The magnets at home are small and the magnet at work is huge.*
How does the author say this idea in several ways?	*The author says that the magnet at work was very different from the magnets at home; the author shows the picture of the huge magnet; Lisa says, "The magnet you use at work is huge!"*
What does the magnetic crane do?	*It sorts metals into two piles: magnetic and nonmagnetic.*
What kind of metal does the crane pick up?	*iron*

Name: _____

Dictionary

Read each word aloud.
Look at the picture or read the definition.

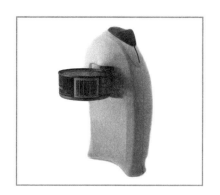

can opener

magnetic crane

aluminum

Words	Definitions
magnificent	very good; excellent
whirred	made a buzzing sound
cabinet	a place to store things
sorts	puts into groups
nonmagnetic	something a magnet will not attract

Write one sentence using two of the words.

_____

_____

Magnificent Magnets

Lisa's kitchen was a busy place. Lisa and her little brother Pete were at the refrigerator. They were looking at it, not in it. That's because the refrigerator had fun magnets: magnetic words and letters. Each morning, Lisa made a silly sentence with the magnetic words.

Pete played with the alphabet magnets. He was happy to find the letters of his name.

Nearby, Dad was making lunch. The can of tuna whirred round and round and then...pop! The lid stuck to the can opener. It had a magnet that held the lid off the can. How useful! Lisa had come across several magnets so far.

"Hey, Dad," said Lisa. "We have magnets all over the kitchen, don't we?"

"Yes, magnets are magnificent," said Dad. He reached for some crackers inside a cabinet. "There's a small magnet in this cabinet door that helps it stay shut. There are magnets all over the house, not just in the kitchen."

Where else had Lisa seen magnets? The shower curtain in the bathroom had little magnets. That's how it stuck to the tub. Lisa also remembered seeing a magnet at her dad's job, but it was very different from the magnets at home.

"The magnet you use at work is huge!" said Lisa.

"Yes, it is!" said Dad. "It's called a magnetic crane. It sorts metal into two piles: magnetic and nonmagnetic. A magnet attracts metals that contain iron. Metals that contain iron are magnetic. The crane leaves behind the nonmagnetic metals. Copper and aluminum are in that pile."

"Cool," said Lisa. "I'll try that. I'll go around the house and sort things into two piles. I'll find magnetic and nonmagnetic objects, like you do."

A magnetic crane sorting metals

Use New Words

Complete each sentence using a word from the word box.
Then read each sentence aloud.

Word Box

| aluminum | cabinet | magnificent |
| nonmagnetic | sorts | whirred |

1 The fan _____ slowly in the hot room.

2 The painting in the museum looked _____.

3 The _____ coins were not attracted to the magnet.

4 We keep classroom supplies in the _____.

5 My dad _____ the clean socks by color.

6 We wrapped the food in _____ foil.

Answer Questions

Read and answer each question.

1 What is the magnet in the kitchen cabinet used for?

   Ⓐ to hang pictures

   Ⓑ to keep it shut

   Ⓒ to sort things

2 What is the biggest difference between Lisa's refrigerator magnets and Dad's magnet at work?

   Ⓐ color

   Ⓑ size

   Ⓒ age

3 Which of these would the magnetic crane pick up?

   Ⓐ refrigerator

   Ⓑ aluminum can

   Ⓒ copper pot

4 What two groups do Dad and Lisa sort things into?

   Ⓐ magnetic and nonmagnetic

   Ⓑ big and small

   Ⓒ steel and iron

5 How are the magnets in Lisa's home useful?

_____

_____

    Reading Paired Text • EMC 1372 • © Evan-Moor Corp.

Write About It

Graphic Organizer

Get a magnet. See if it attracts the objects below.
Write what happens. Then add one more object.

	Magnetic or nonmagnetic?

Writing Prompt

Are all metals magnetic? Explain your answer.

_____

_____

_____

Understanding Magnets

Topic: Understanding Magnets
Big Question: Does a magnet stick to all shiny things?

Tie It Together

Use the script below to guide students in discussing the Big Question and what they have learned about the topic from the paired selections.

Questions	Sample Responses
According to the selections, magnets can be big or small. What are some examples of big and small magnets?	*Small magnets: refrigerator magnets, magnet on the can opener, magnets in the shower curtain. Big magnet: magnetic crane.*
What kinds of things are magnetic?	*refrigerator, paper clip, pin, nail, car*
In both selections, magnets are used to keep doors shut. Tell about these doors.	*In "What Will a Magnet Attract?" a magnet holds a refrigerator door shut. In "Magnificent Magnets," a magnet holds a kitchen cabinet shut.*
What are some magnetic things here in the classroom? And at home?	*Answers should reflect examples given in the selections.*
In "What Will a Magnet Attract?" what kind of metal does a magnet attract? What metal does it not attract?	*A magnet will attract metal that has iron in it. A magnet will not attract coins.*
In "Magnificent Magnets," what is the purpose of the magnetic crane at Dad's work?	*It sorts metals into magnetic and nonmagnetic piles.*
Our Big Question was "Does a magnet stick to all shiny things?" How did "What Will a Magnet Attract?" answer this question?	*"What Will a Magnet Attract?" shows that a magnet will not stick to all shiny things. Coins and glass are shiny, but a magnet will not stick to them.*
How did "Magnificent Magnets" answer it?	*In "Magnificent Magnets," the crane sorts shiny metals into magnetic and nonmagnetic piles. That means some shiny metals, like aluminum, are not magnetic.*

Plan Your Writing

Draw or write your answers.

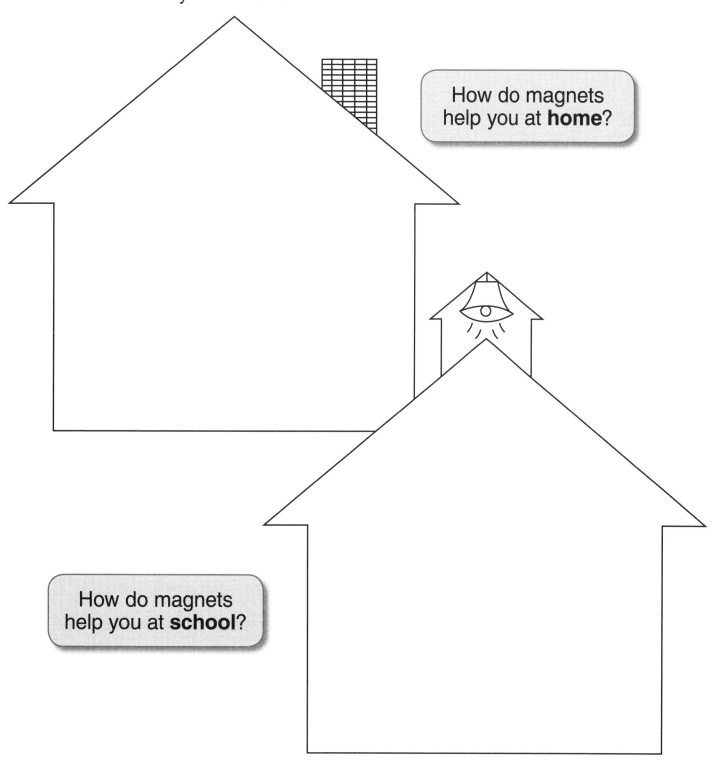

How do magnets help you at **home**?

How do magnets help you at **school**?

Write a Paragraph

Writing Prompt

You read about different uses for magnets.
Explain how magnets help us. Use words from the word box.

Word Box

fun	helps	huge	lift
power	silly	stick	strong

_____

_____

_____

_____

_____

_____

_____

_____

_____

_____

_____

We Help Each Other

Student Objective: Students will see how stories from two different cultures convey the same message about working together.

Big Question:

How can we help each other?

Topic Introduction: Explain that in all parts of the world, people cooperate with each other. Tell students they will read two selections—one from the United States and one from Mexico—that have the same message about people in communities who help each other.

Paired Text Selections:

Assessment Materials:

Lesson Plan

1. Introduce the Selection

Tell students that they are going to read a folk tale that is told all over the world. The setting is different in each country, but the message is always the same. It is a message about working together, or sharing what we have, to make something good.

2. Learn New Vocabulary: Dictionary

Reproduce the Dictionary page and distribute it to each student. Read aloud each pictured word as you point to it. Have students echo you as they also point to each word. Ask students to identify the two words in the bigger word *campfire*. For defined vocabulary, read the definitions aloud. Have volunteers use each word in a sentence. Call attention to the unusual use of the words *answer* and *eyed*.

Have students write a sentence using two of the words. Then have students find each vocabulary word in the selection and read the context sentence.

3. Read the Selection

Reproduce the selection and distribute it to each student. Have students follow along silently as you read aloud. Direct students' attention to graphic elements or visual aids. Then have students read the selection independently, with a partner, or in small groups.

4. Apply Vocabulary: Use New Words

Reproduce the Use New Words page and distribute it to each student. Have students complete the activity independently, with a partner, or in small groups.

5. Analyze the Selection: Oral Close Reading Activity

Guide students in a discussion about the selection using the script on the following page. Explain that close reading will help them notice important parts of the selection. Encourage students to refer to the selection as necessary to find information.

To support visual learners, you may wish to cover up the sample responses and reproduce and distribute the discussion questions for students to refer to.

6. Understand the Selection: Answer Questions

Reproduce the Answer Questions page and distribute it to each student. Have students complete the activity. Encourage them to refer to the selection as necessary to help them answer questions and/or to check their answers.

You may wish to use this as a formative assessment to determine students' understanding of the text.

7. Write About the Selection: Write About It

Reproduce the Write About It page and distribute it to each student. Have students brainstorm in small groups and complete the writing assignment collaboratively or independently.

Oral Close Reading Activity

Ask students the following text-dependent questions and have them refer to the selection as necessary.

Questions	Sample Responses
During what time of the year does this story take place?	*autumn*
Was the farmer stingy?	*yes*
What does the farmer say to show his stinginess?	*"I don't give food to strangers" and "I'll give you a stone and some water, but that's it."*
Who was the first person to ask about the hiker's stone soup?	*the farmer's wife*
What did she donate?	*an onion*
In what way was the hiker lucky that the farmer had three daughters and four sons?	*The hiker was lucky that the farmer had many children because each of them was happy to donate something to the soup.*
According to the story, what did the soup contain?	*onion, carrot, celery, tomato, potato, garlic, corn, salt, and a stone*
What trick did the hiker play on the family?	*He was not really making stone soup. He tricked them into each giving a vegetable for the soup, and he made vegetable soup.*

Dictionary

Read each word aloud.
Look at the picture or read the definition.

campfire

onion

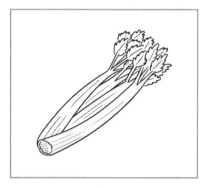
celery

Words	Definitions
answer	to react or move when you hear a door knock or a phone ring
stingy	not wanting to share
eyed	looked at closely
generous	willing to share
donate	to give something
luckily	by good luck

Write one sentence using two of the words.

_____

_____

Stone Soup

One cool autumn day, a hiker knocked on a farmer's door. The farmer took a long time to answer. Finally, he opened the door just a crack.

"Excuse me, sir," said the hiker. "I am lost, and I ran out of food yesterday."

"I don't give food to strangers," said the stingy farmer, about to close the door.

"Please," said the hiker. "I'm not begging for food. I just want to borrow a stone from your garden. I need to fill my pot with water, too."

The farmer eyed the hiker. "Fine," he answered at last. "I'll give you a stone and some water, but that's it."

The hiker thanked the farmer. He filled the pot with water. He washed the dirt off the stone and put it into the pot. Then he set the pot on a small campfire. Soon the water was boiling. The farmer's wife came to see what was going on. "I've never seen anyone make soup out of a stone and water," she said.

77

"It will be delicious," smiled the hiker, "but it would be better with an onion."

"I have an onion," said the farmer's wife. She went to the house for an onion, and the hiker dropped it into the pot.

The farmer's daughter came to see what was cooking. "I've never seen soup made out of a stone, onion, and water," she said.

"It will be delicious. But it would be even better with a carrot," said the hiker. The daughter was very generous. She was happy to donate a carrot.

Luckily, the farmer had three daughters and four sons. Each one came by, one after another, to see what was cooking. And each one donated something new. In the end, the soup had onion, carrot, celery, tomato, potato, garlic, corn, and salt. And a stone, of course.

The hiker was right: stone soup is delicious!

Use New Words

Complete each sentence using a word from the word box.
Then read each sentence aloud.

Word Box

answer	donate	eyed
generous	luckily	stingy

1 Kim is so _____. She wouldn't let me have
part of her lunch.

2 My sister is _____. She always shares her food.

3 I let the phone ring three times, then I _____ it.

4 _____, it stopped raining by noon.

5 We can _____ some of our toys to the
children.

6 I _____ the red bird until it flew away.

Answer Questions

Read and answer each question.

1 What was the first vegetable to go in the soup?

Ⓐ carrot

Ⓑ onion

Ⓒ stone

2 The opposite of **generous** is _____.

Ⓐ delicious

Ⓑ donate

Ⓒ stingy

3 Which sentence uses **answer** in the same way as the story?

Ⓐ Please answer yes or no.

Ⓑ Write the best answer.

Ⓒ Please answer the door.

4 Which word tells about the farmer?

Ⓐ stingy

Ⓑ generous

Ⓒ happy

5 Did the farmer treat the hiker the same as his wife and children did?

_____

_____

Name: _____

Write About It

Graphic Organizer

Write the recipe for stone soup.
First, list the ingredients (what you need).
Then tell how to make it (what you do).

Stone Soup

What you need:

- 1 pot of water
- _____
- _____
- _____
- _____

- _____
- _____
- _____
- _____

What you do:

_____

_____

_____

_____

_____

_____

Lesson Plan

1. Introduce the Selection

Help students think of what it takes to prepare for a party. Then tell students that they are going to read a story about a couple who gets help from the community to make their wedding day special.

2. Learn New Vocabulary: Dictionary

Reproduce the Dictionary page and distribute it to each student. Read aloud each pictured word as you point to it. Have students echo you as they also point to each word. Have students describe the relationship between merchant and customer. For defined vocabulary, read the definitions aloud. Have volunteers use each word in a sentence.

Have students write a sentence using two of the words. Then have students find each vocabulary word in the selection and read the context sentence.

3. Read the Selection

Reproduce the selection and distribute it to each student. Have students follow along silently as you read aloud. Direct students' attention to graphic elements or visual aids. Then have students read the selection independently, with a partner, or in small groups.

4. Apply Vocabulary: Use New Words

Reproduce the Use New Words page and distribute it to each student. Have students complete the activity independently, with a partner, or in small groups.

5. Analyze the Selection: Oral Close Reading Activity

Guide students in a discussion about the selection using the script on the following page. Explain that close reading will help them notice important parts of the selection. Encourage students to refer to the selection as necessary to find information.

To support visual learners, you may wish to cover up the sample responses and reproduce and distribute the discussion questions for students to refer to.

6. Understand the Selection: Answer Questions

Reproduce the Answer Questions page and distribute it to each student. Have students complete the activity. Encourage them to refer to the selection as necessary to help them answer questions and/or to check their answers.

You may wish to use this as a formative assessment to determine students' understanding of the text.

7. Write About the Selection: Write About It

Reproduce the Write About It page and distribute it to each student. Have students brainstorm in small groups and complete the writing assignment collaboratively or independently.

Oral Close Reading Activity

Ask students the following text-dependent questions and have them refer to the selection as necessary.

Questions	Sample Responses
Why didn't Sergio and Magda have a wedding reception?	*They had no family and no money.*
According to the story, what was the one small thing missing?	*a wedding cake*
In what country does the story take place?	*Mexico*
What special celebration was happening in the village?	*a celebration of the Feast of San Juan*
How are they celebrating?	*with a parade*
Who was the first merchant marching in the parade?	*Mr. Blanco*
What does he do for a living?	*He sells butter.*
Why didn't Panadero Bakery have any customers?	*The customers were all at the parade.*

Dictionary

Read each word aloud.
Look at the picture or read the definition.

merchant

dough

customer

Words	Definitions
reception	a party for a wedding
feast	a large meal
spectators	people watching a parade or other event
capture	to catch
littered	covered
exchange	something given for something else

Write one sentence using two of the words.

_____

_____

Mexican Wedding Cakes

One summer day, in a village in central Mexico, Sergio and Magda got married. They had no family and no money, so they had no wedding reception. Still, they were happy. Just one thing was missing.

"I wish we had a wedding cake," said Magda. "Even a little one."

It just so happened that the couple was married on June 24, on the Feast of San Juan. To celebrate, merchants paraded down Main Street. This year, the first merchant was Mr. Blanco. He sold butter, and he passed out samples from a large pail. He handed Sergio a paper cone with a bit of butter at the bottom.

The second merchant was Mr. Panadero, the village baker. He tossed powdered sugar toward the spectators. It fluttered like snowflakes. Children squealed in delight. Sergio opened his cone and lifted it to capture some sugar. Sergio closed the cone and mixed the sugar and butter together. This gave Sergio an idea. Magda would have her cake!

On the other side of the street, Mr. Panadero's wife was tossing out flour. Sergio crossed over to that side and lifted his cone, catching a fistful of flour. He mixed the flour, sugar, and butter.

Magda and Sergio walked to a walnut tree nearby. Hundreds of walnuts littered the ground. Sergio smashed some against a rock and added the ground nuts to the flour, sugar, and butter. He made a stiff dough, which he rolled into three little balls. The couple walked to Panadero Bakery. Mr. Panadero's youngest son was there, but not a single customer. They were all at the parade.

"I see you are baking bread," said Sergio. "May I put these three wedding cakes in the oven, along with your bread? It will only take ten minutes. I will give you one of the wedding cakes as a trade."

"That's a fair exchange," said the young Panadero. "I have never seen wedding cakes like this. I wonder what they taste like."

"I made them as a gift for my new wife. I don't know how they taste, either," said Sergio. "We will find out."

When the cakes came out of the oven, they were not pretty. In fact, they looked like stones. The generous Panadero dusted them with powdered sugar to look like tiny snowballs. He wished Sergio and Magda a long and happy life. They all enjoyed the buttery Mexican wedding cakes together.

Use New Words

Complete each sentence using a word from the word box.
Then read each sentence aloud.

Word Box		
capture	exchange	feast
littered	reception	spectators

1 Papers fell out of the bag and _____ the street.

2 The _____ all clapped for the winner.

3 The wedding _____ was in a garden.

4 The mice had a _____ with the extra food.

5 The pants were too small, so the store gave us an

_____ for a bigger size.

6 I tried to _____ the butterfly with my net.

Answer Questions

Read and answer each question.

1 What problem do Sergio and Magda have?

   Ⓐ They don't have a wedding cake.

   Ⓑ They can't get married.

   Ⓒ Nobody came to their wedding.

2 What are the ingredients in Mexican wedding cakes?

   Ⓐ butter, eggs, flour, nuts

   Ⓑ butter, sugar, flour, nuts

   Ⓒ butter, sugar, eggs, flour

3 Where did Sergio and Magda get the nuts for the cakes?

   Ⓐ from a tree

   Ⓑ from a farmer

   Ⓒ from a baker

4 How does the young Panadero help the couple?

   Ⓐ He sings them a wedding song.

   Ⓑ He gives them money.

   Ⓒ He lets them use his oven.

5 How do the townspeople help to make Magda's wish come true?

_____

_____

Name: _____

Write About It

Graphic Organizer

Write or draw the ingredients for Mexican wedding cakes in the small circles. Write the steps to make the cakes in the large circle.

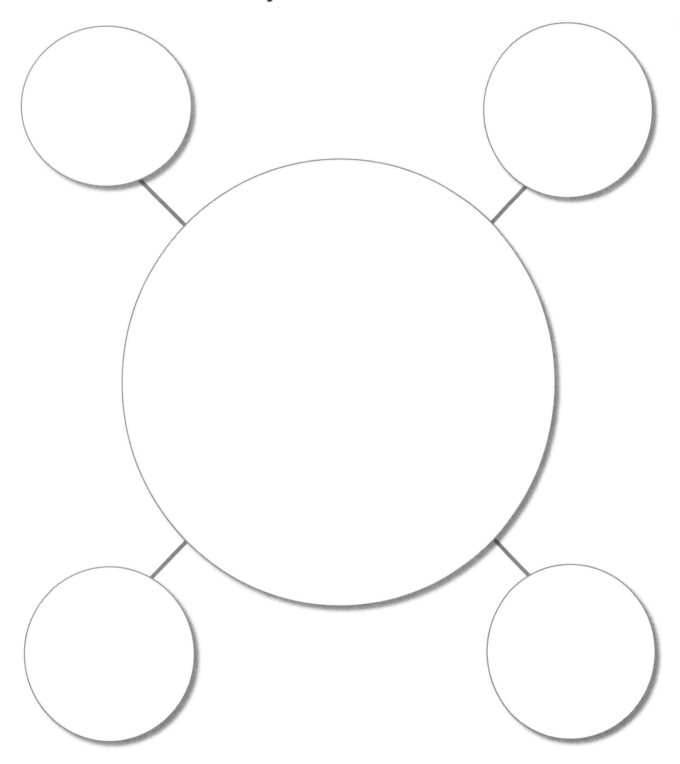

We Help Each Other

Topic: We Help Each Other
Big Question: How can we help each other?

Tie It Together

Use the script below to guide students in discussing the Big Question and what they have learned about the topic from the paired selections.

Questions	Sample Responses
What is the same about the hiker and Sergio?	*They are both poor; they both take ingredients from other people and make something good to eat.*
What is the main idea of both stories?	*If we each donate a little, we can make something good.*
How is the hiker different from Sergio?	*The hiker tricks the farmer's family into giving him food, but Sergio gets samples from the merchants in the parade. The hiker is by himself, but Sergio has a wife.*
How is the setting of each story different?	*The setting of "Stone Soup" is a farm during autumn, and the setting of "Mexican Wedding Cakes" is a Mexican village during summer.*
Think about the titles of both stories. How are the titles similar? How are they different?	*The titles refer to the name of the food that is made in the stories. They are different because one is a soup and one is a type of cake.*
Our Big Question was "How can we help each other?" How did both selections answer this question?	*In both selections, people help each other by donating ingredients to make something. In "Stone Soup," people donate vegetables to make soup. In "Mexican Wedding Cakes," people donate ingredients to make cakes.*

Plan Your Writing

Fill in the chart.
Look back at the two selections if you need to.

	Stone Soup	Mexican Wedding Cakes
Who needs something?		
What problems do they have getting it?		
Who gives something?		
What do they donate?		
What happens in the end?		

Write a Paragraph

Writing Prompt

Pretend you are the hiker, Sergio, or Magda.
Write a thank-you note to the people who helped you.
Then decorate your note.

Dear _____ ,

Thank you for the _____

_____

_____

_____

_____

_____

_____

_____

Sincerely,

_____

Unit Overview
National Memorials

Student Objective: Students will recognize the significance of national memorials.

Big Question:

How do national memorials help us remember history?

Topic Introduction: Explain that a national memorial is an area in the United States that helps us remember important people or events. Tell students that they will read about two national memorials located in South Dakota.

Paired Text Selections:

Selection: *Mount Rushmore*
Nonfiction, Level J

Teacher Pages:

Student Pages:

Selection: *Colossal Crazy Horse*
Nonfiction, Level L

Teacher Pages:

Student Pages:

Assessment Materials:

Teacher Page: (Paired Text Discussion)

Student Pages: (Reproduce and distribute one copy to each student.)

Lesson Plan

1. **Introduce the Selection**

   Have students tell what they know about George Washington, Thomas Jefferson, Theodore Roosevelt, and Abraham Lincoln. Tell students that they are going to read a nonfiction selection about Mount Rushmore, a national memorial which features the faces of these four presidents.

2. **Learn New Vocabulary: Dictionary**

   Reproduce the Dictionary page and distribute it to each student. Read aloud each pictured word as you point to it. Have students echo you as they also point to each word. For defined vocabulary, read the definitions aloud. Have volunteers use each word in a sentence. Focus on *national*, *symbolize*, and *equality*, calling attention to the suffixes. Discuss how the suffix affects the meaning of each root word.

   Have students write a sentence using two of the words. Then have students find each vocabulary word in the selection and read the context sentence.

3. **Read the Selection**

   Reproduce the selection and distribute it to each student. Have students follow along silently as you read aloud. Direct students' attention to graphic elements or visual aids. Then have students read the selection independently, with a partner, or in small groups.

4. **Apply Vocabulary: Use New Words**

   Reproduce the Use New Words page and distribute it to each student. Have students complete the activity independently, with a partner, or in small groups.

5. **Analyze the Selection: Oral Close Reading Activity**

   Guide students in a discussion about the selection using the script on the following page. Explain that close reading will help them notice important parts of the selection. Encourage students to refer to the selection as necessary to find information.

   To support visual learners, you may wish to cover up the sample responses and reproduce and distribute the discussion questions for students to refer to.

6. **Understand the Selection: Answer Questions**

   Reproduce the Answer Questions page and distribute it to each student. Have students complete the activity. Encourage them to refer to the selection as necessary to help them answer questions and/or to check their answers.

   You may wish to use this as a formative assessment to determine students' understanding of the text.

7. **Write About the Selection: Write About It**

   Reproduce the Write About It page and distribute it to each student. Have students brainstorm in small groups and complete the writing assignment collaboratively or independently.

Oral Close Reading Activity

Ask students the following text-dependent questions and have them refer to the selection as necessary.

Questions	Sample Responses
In which state is Mount Rushmore located?	*South Dakota*
Why is Mount Rushmore called a memorial?	*because it helps us to remember the four presidents*
Why was Gutzon Borglum important to Mount Rushmore?	*He was the artist who carved Mount Rushmore.*
What happened to Borglum before the memorial was finished?	*He died, and his son had to finish it.*
What is special about the four presidents on Mount Rushmore?	*They did important things. George Washington was the first president. Thomas Jefferson wrote the Declaration of Independence. Theodore Roosevelt helped set up national forests. Abraham Lincoln ended slavery in America.*
According to the text, what can you learn at Mount Rushmore?	*You can learn about American history. You can learn about the state flags. You can learn about presidents. You can learn about the plants and animals of South Dakota.*
How does the author compare a bald eagle to Mount Rushmore?	*They are both national symbols.*

Name: _____

Dictionary

Read each word aloud.
Look at the picture or read the definition.

mount

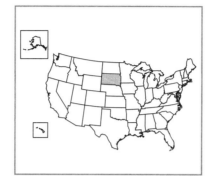
South Dakota

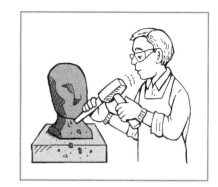
carve

Words	Definitions
national	belonging to a country
memorial	something built to remember someone
landmark	an important place or building
symbolize	to stand for; to represent
equality	having the same rights
native	something that belongs to a place

Write one sentence using two of the words.

_____

_____

Reading Paired Text • EMC 1372 • © Evan-Moor Corp.

Mount Rushmore

From left to right: George Washington, Thomas Jefferson, Theodore Roosevelt, and Abraham Lincoln

Mount Rushmore National Memorial is a landmark in South Dakota. In 1927, an artist named Gutzon Borglum began carving this national memorial. Borglum died before the memorial was completed, but his son finished it. It took 14 years to carve. The memorial has the faces of four presidents carved in rock. They are George Washington, Thomas Jefferson, Theodore Roosevelt, and Abraham Lincoln.

These presidents were chosen for what they symbolize. George Washington was our first president. Thomas Jefferson wrote the Declaration of Independence. Theodore Roosevelt helped set up national forests so we could enjoy them. Abraham Lincoln ended slavery in America. He represents equality for all.

Each year, over three million people visit Mount Rushmore. You can learn a lot about American history here. You can walk along the Avenue of Flags and see a flag for each of the 50 states. You can walk the Presidential Trail. It leads to the base of the mountain. Here, you can see the presidents up close. Along the trail, you can see plants and animals native to South Dakota. You may even get to see a bald eagle. It represents strength and freedom. The bald eagle is a national symbol, just like Mount Rushmore.

Use New Words

Complete each sentence using a word from the word box.
Then read each sentence aloud.

Word Box

equality	landmark	memorial
national	native	symbolize

1 A heart can _____ love or friendship.

2 Red, white, and blue are the _____ colors.

3 On _____ Day, we remember people who died in wars.

4 All students should be treated with _____.

5 My friend Monica is a _____ of Brazil.

6 The Statue of Liberty is a famous _____.

Answer Questions

Read and answer each question.

1 Mount Rushmore is made of _____.

   Ⓐ metal

   Ⓑ rock

   Ⓒ wood

2 Theodore Roosevelt is famous for _____.

   Ⓐ writing the Declaration of Independence

   Ⓑ creating the national forests

   Ⓒ being the first president

3 Abraham Lincoln represents _____.

   Ⓐ conservation

   Ⓑ education

   Ⓒ equality

4 How can you get to the base of the mountain?

   Ⓐ Walk the Presidential Trail.

   Ⓑ Walk along the Avenue of Flags.

   Ⓒ Follow the bald eagle.

5 How are a bald eagle and Mount Rushmore the same?

_____

_____

Name: _____

Write About It

Graphic Organizer

Write the name of each president.
Then write why each president was chosen for the monument.

Lesson Plan

1. **Introduce the Selection**

   Brainstorm things that are colossal, such as a dinosaur, a whale, or a volcano. Then tell students that they are going to read a story about a colossal monument called Crazy Horse. The monument is carved into a mountain in South Dakota.

2. **Learn New Vocabulary: Dictionary**

   Reproduce the Dictionary page and distribute it to each student. Read aloud each pictured word as you point to it. Have students echo you as they also point to each word. For defined vocabulary, read the definitions aloud. Guide students in finding the synonyms. (*sculpture, carving*) Have volunteers use each word in a sentence.

   Have students write a sentence using two of the words. Then have students find each vocabulary word in the selection and read the context sentence.

3. **Read the Selection**

   Reproduce the selection and distribute it to each student. Have students follow along silently as you read aloud. Direct students' attention to graphic elements or visual aids. Then have students read the selection independently, with a partner, or in small groups.

4. **Apply Vocabulary: Use New Words**

   Reproduce the Use New Words page and distribute it to each student. Have students complete the activity independently, with a partner, or in small groups.

5. **Analyze the Selection: Oral Close Reading Activity**

   Guide students in a discussion about the selection using the script on the following page. Explain that close reading will help them notice important parts of the selection. Encourage students to refer to the selection as necessary to find information.

   To support visual learners, you may wish to cover up the sample responses and reproduce and distribute the discussion questions for students to refer to.

6. **Understand the Selection: Answer Questions**

   Reproduce the Answer Questions page and distribute it to each student. Have students complete the activity. Encourage them to refer to the selection as necessary to help them answer questions and/or to check their answers.

   You may wish to use this as a formative assessment to determine students' understanding of the text.

7. **Write About the Selection: Write About It**

   Reproduce the Write About It page and distribute it to each student. Have students brainstorm in small groups and complete the writing assignment collaboratively or independently.

Oral Close Reading Activity

Ask students the following text-dependent questions and have them refer to the selection as necessary.

Questions	Sample Responses
In which state is the Crazy Horse Memorial located?	*South Dakota*
What other memorial is nearby?	*Mount Rushmore*
Memorials honor important people. Who does the Crazy Horse Memorial honor?	*the Lakota chief, Crazy Horse; Native Americans, especially the Lakota people*
Before he started carving the Crazy Horse Memorial, what was the artist's first step?	*He made a sketch of what he wanted it to look like.*
What words tell about the Crazy Horse Memorial?	*bigger, colossal, largest, honor*
What part will be carved next?	*the horse's head*
When will the Crazy Horse Memorial be finished?	*No one knows for sure when it will be finished.*

Name: _____

Dictionary

Read each word aloud.
Look at the picture or read the definition.

Mount Rushmore

sculpture

sketch

Words	Definitions
colossal	big; huge
carving	a figure cut out of stone or wood
honor	to like; to treat in a special way
Lakota	Native Americans from South Dakota
monument	something built to honor an important person
chip away	to take away a little at a time

Write one sentence using two of the words.

_____

_____

Colossal Crazy Horse

South Dakota is famous for Mount Rushmore, the huge carving of four presidents. Nearby, there's another mountain carving. This one will be even bigger than Mount Rushmore. It's colossal! When it is finished, it will be the largest sculpture in the world. It's called the Crazy Horse Memorial.

Memorials honor important people. The Crazy Horse Memorial is a way to honor Native Americans, especially the Lakota people. They lived in the area that is now South Dakota. The Lakota people had a chief named Crazy Horse. He was a kind leader. They wanted a monument to remember him by.

They invited an artist named Korczak Ziolkowski to make the monument. First he made a sketch of the chief on horseback, with his arm pointing. Ziolkowski began carving the mountain in 1948.

This is what the Crazy Horse Memorial looked like in 2012.

He used special tools to chip away at the rock. He worked alone for many years. He died in 1982, before he could finish the face of the chief. Ziolkowski's wife and seven of his children continued carving. They are still chipping away at the mountain today. The horse's head will be next. It will be huge. All four of the Mount Rushmore faces would fit inside this horse's head!

When will the monument be finished? No one knows for sure. Until then, the Ziolkowski family will continue to chip away.

This painting shows what the memorial will look like when it is finished.

Use New Words

Complete each sentence using a word from the word box.
Then read each sentence aloud.

Word Box

carving	chip away	colossal
honor	Lakota	monument

1 We _____ our grandparents.

2 Dad made a _____ out of wood.

3 King Kong is a _____ gorilla.

4 The ants will _____ at the muffin.

5 People made a _____ to their hero.

6 Crazy Horse was a _____ leader.

Answer Questions

Read and answer each question.

1 The Crazy Horse Memorial will be _____ than Mount Rushmore.

Ⓐ bigger

Ⓑ smaller

Ⓒ shorter

2 Which words show that the Crazy Horse Memorial will be colossal?

Ⓐ The Crazy Horse Memorial honors Native Americans.

Ⓑ The Mount Rushmore faces would fit inside this horse's head.

Ⓒ Ziolkowski began carving the mountain in 1948.

3 Crazy Horse was a _____.

Ⓐ president

Ⓑ artist

Ⓒ chief

4 Why is the Crazy Horse Memorial important?

Ⓐ It honors a Lakota chief.

Ⓑ It is still not finished.

Ⓒ It is being carved by a family.

5 How would you describe the Crazy Horse Memorial to someone who has never seen it?

_____

_____

Reading Paired Text • EMC 1372 • © Evan-Moor Corp.

Write About It

Pretend that the Crazy Horse Memorial is finally finished.
Draw a sign to welcome visitors to the monument.
Write why Crazy Horse was important.
Tell about the artist and his family.

Welcome to the Crazy Horse Memorial

National Memorials

Topic: National Memorials
Big Question: How do national memorials help us remember history?

Tie It Together

Use the script below to guide students in discussing the Big Question and what they have learned about the topic from the paired selections.

Questions	Sample Responses
Where are the memorials in the selections located?	*in South Dakota*
How is the Crazy Horse Memorial different from Mount Rushmore?	*Crazy Horse is still not finished; Crazy Horse shows a Lakota chief and Mount Rushmore shows four presidents.*
What is the same about the two artists mentioned in the selections?	*The artists' children continued carving the memorials after the artists died.*
The two monuments symbolize different things. How would you describe what each monument symbolizes?	*Mount Rushmore symbolizes the birth of a nation, independence, forests, equality, and freedom. The Crazy Horse Memorial symbolizes Native American culture.*
Our Big Question was "How do national memorials help us remember history?" How did "Mount Rushmore" answer this question?	*Mount Rushmore helps us remember four important presidents and what they did for the country.*
How did "Colossal Crazy Horse" answer it?	*Crazy Horse helps us remember a Native American chief. This monument helps us remember the first inhabitants of this country.*

Plan Your Writing

You read about two national memorials.
Write how they are different and the same.
Use the diagram to help you.

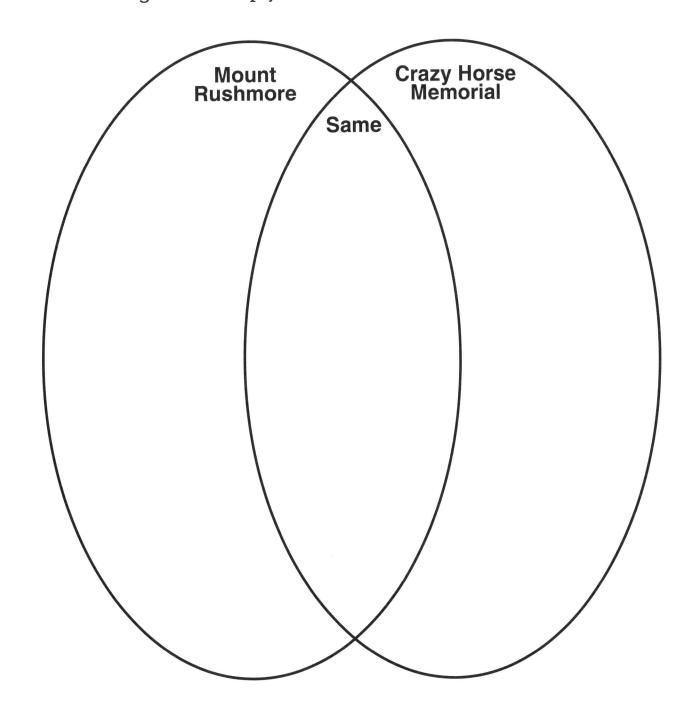

Mount Rushmore   Same   Crazy Horse Memorial

Write a Paragraph

Writing Prompt

Write a paragraph that tells tourists which monument in South Dakota they should visit. Give your reasons.

_____

_____

_____

_____

_____

_____

_____

_____

_____

_____

_____

_____

_____

_____

People Can Change the World

Student Objective: Students will recognize the contributions of two American heroes.

Big Question:

Do I have the power to change the world?

Topic Introduction: Explain that ordinary people have the power to make important changes in the world. Tell students they will read selections about two American heroes who used peaceful methods to help people.

Paired Text Selections:

Assessment Materials:

Lesson Plan

1. Introduce the Selection

Ask students to think of big fields where fruits and vegetables are grown by many hardworking people. Tell students that they are going to read a historical article about Cesar Chavez, a leader who helped improve working conditions for American farmworkers.

2. Learn New Vocabulary: Dictionary

Reproduce the Dictionary page and distribute it to each student. Read aloud each pictured word as you point to it. Have students echo you as they also point to each word. Emphasize the spelling pattern *ought* in the word *drought*. Point out that the word *march* can be a verb or a noun: *We will march in a march.* For defined vocabulary, read the definitions aloud. Have volunteers use each word in a sentence.

Have students write a sentence using two of the words. Then have students find each vocabulary word in the selection and read the context sentence.

3. Read the Selection

Reproduce the selection and distribute it to each student. Have students follow along silently as you read aloud. Direct students' attention to graphic elements or visual aids. Then have students read the selection independently, with a partner, or in small groups.

4. Apply Vocabulary: Use New Words

Reproduce the Use New Words page and distribute it to each student. Have students complete the activity independently, with a partner, or in small groups.

5. Analyze the Selection: Oral Close Reading Activity

Guide students in a discussion about the selection using the script on the following page. Explain that close reading will help them notice important parts of the selection. Encourage students to refer to the selection as necessary to find information.

To support visual learners, you may wish to cover up the sample responses and reproduce and distribute the discussion questions for students to refer to.

6. Understand the Selection: Answer Questions

Reproduce the Answer Questions page and distribute it to each student. Have students complete the activity. Encourage them to refer to the selection as necessary to help them answer questions and/or to check their answers.

You may wish to use this as a formative assessment to determine students' understanding of the text.

7. Write About the Selection: Write About It

Reproduce the Write About It page and distribute it to each student. Have students brainstorm in small groups and complete the writing assignment collaboratively or independently.

Oral Close Reading Activity

Ask students the following text-dependent questions and have them refer to the selection as necessary.

Questions	Sample Responses
What happened to the Chavez farm?	*A drought dried up all the crops.*
A migrant worker does not stay in one place very long. What detail tells more about this main idea?	*Chavez attended over 30 schools!*
In what ways was farm work difficult?	*Workers were paid very little. Sometimes they had to live in run-down camps without clean water.*
Whose example did Cesar Chavez follow?	*Dr. Martin Luther King, Jr.*
What did Chavez do that was similar to what Dr. King had done?	*He and the workers marched so that people would help them make a change.*
What happened when people stopped buying grapes?	*The grape growers finally listened to the workers.*
What year did Cesar Chavez die?	*1993*

Dictionary

Read each word aloud.
Look at the picture or read the definition.

drought

run-down

march

Words	Definitions
boycott	a decision not to buy something
migrant	a person who travels from one place to another looking for work
nonviolent	peaceful
wages	money people get paid for working
improve	to make better

Write one sentence using two of the words.

_____

_____

Reading Paired Text • EMC 1372 • © Evan-Moor Corp.

Chavez and the Grape Boycott

Cesar Chavez was born in Yuma, Arizona, in 1927. His family owned a small farm and a grocery store. When Cesar was ten years old, a drought destroyed his family's farm. There was no rain, and the crops dried up.

The family moved to California to start over. They became migrant farm workers. They went from farm to farm looking for work. They never stayed in one place very long. In fact, Cesar attended over 30 schools! In eighth grade, he left school to help his family by picking grapes. Farm work was hard. Workers were paid very little money. Sometimes they had to live in run-down camps without clean water.

Cesar Chavez felt the workers should have a better life. He remembered that Dr. Martin Luther King, Jr., had led nonviolent marches. The marches got people to listen. Chavez decided to help the farm workers. Chavez asked the workers to stop working and to march with him. In 1965, they marched to demand fair wages and safe working conditions. Chavez got another idea. He asked people to stop buying grapes. He hoped this boycott would make the grape growers listen.

The boycott and the marches worked. People all over the United States stopped buying grapes. By 1970, the growers finally gave the workers what they wanted. The growers made changes. Some of the changes became laws in California. Cesar was an ordinary man who made big changes happen. Until his death in 1993, Chavez worked to improve the lives of farm workers.

Chavez (front, center) leads a march in Coachella, California, around 1991.

Use New Words

Complete each sentence using a word from the word box.
Then read each sentence aloud.

Word Box		
boycott	improve	march
migrant	nonviolent	wages

1 The _____ worker is picking grapes in the field.

2 Our school is going to _____ in the parade.

3 If I study hard, my grades will _____.

4 Some people make good _____ for their work.

5 Let's find _____ ways to solve our problems.

6 People organized a _____ of the restaurant, and the owners lost money.

Answer Questions

Read and answer each question.

1 A drought can destroy crops by _____.

   Ⓐ making them too wet

   Ⓑ drying them up

   Ⓒ blowing them away

2 A run-down house is _____.

   Ⓐ brand new

   Ⓑ standing tall

   Ⓒ falling apart

3 Which sentence uses **fair** in the same way as the text?

   Ⓐ My fair skin burns easily in the sun.

   Ⓑ We rode the Ferris wheel at the fair.

   Ⓒ It's not fair that my sister gets a new bike.

4 Which word tells about the farm workers' marches?

   Ⓐ peaceful

   Ⓑ angry

   Ⓒ small

5 In what way did Americans help the farm workers?

_____

_____

Write About It

Write about the grape boycott on the grapes below.
Tell who, what, where, when, why, and how.

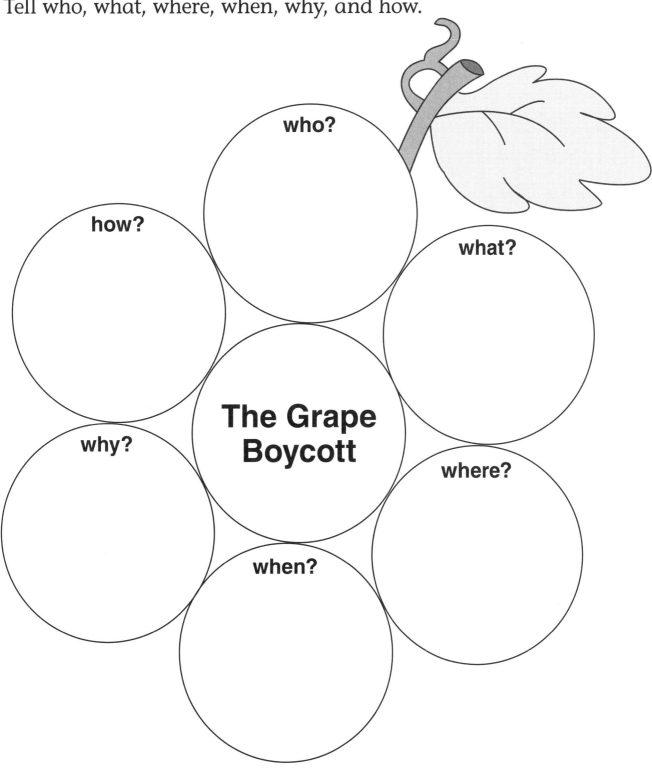

Lesson Plan

1. Introduce the Selection

Ask students what they know about Martin Luther King, Jr. Tell them that they are going to read a nonfiction article about Martin Luther King, Jr., a leader who used nonviolent methods to improve the lives of Americans, in particular black Americans.

**2. Learn New Vocabulary:
Dictionary**

Reproduce the Dictionary page and distribute it to each student. Read aloud each pictured word as you point to it. Have students echo you as they also point to each word. For defined vocabulary, read the definitions aloud. Have volunteers use each word in a sentence. Point out the word *injustice*, and have students identify the prefix that means "not" or "the opposite of." (*in-*)

Have students write a sentence using two of the words. Then have students find each vocabulary word in the selection and read the context sentence.

3. Read the Selection

Reproduce the selection and distribute it to each student. Have students follow along silently as you read aloud. Direct students' attention to graphic elements or visual aids. Then have students read the selection independently, with a partner, or in small groups.

**4. Apply Vocabulary:
Use New Words**

Reproduce the Use New Words page and distribute it to each student. Have students complete the activity independently, with a partner, or in small groups.

**5. Analyze the Selection:
Oral Close Reading Activity**

Guide students in a discussion about the selection using the script on the following page. Explain that close reading will help them notice important parts of the selection. Encourage students to refer to the selection as necessary to find information.

To support visual learners, you may wish to cover up the sample responses and reproduce and distribute the discussion questions for students to refer to.

**6. Understand the Selection:
Answer Questions**

Reproduce the Answer Questions page and distribute it to each student. Have students complete the activity. Encourage them to refer to the selection as necessary to help them answer questions and/or to check their answers.

You may wish to use this as a formative assessment to determine students' understanding of the text.

**7. Write About the Selection:
Write About It**

Reproduce the Write About It page and distribute it to each student. Have students brainstorm in small groups and complete the writing assignment collaboratively or independently.

Oral Close Reading Activity

Ask students the following text-dependent questions and have them refer to the selection as necessary.

Questions	Sample Responses
What detail shows that King was a good student?	*He went to college early, when he was only 15 years old.*
According to the text, what two groups of people were not treated fairly?	*people in India and black people in the United States*
Whose example did Martin Luther King follow?	*Mahatma Gandhi*
What words from the text tell about Mahatma Gandhi?	*peaceful, helped, nonviolent*
What did King do that was the same?	*He used nonviolent methods, such as a boycott, to make changes.*
What happened when black people stopped riding the buses?	*The bus companies lost money.*
What happened after they lost money?	*The laws were changed and buses were integrated.*
Rosa Parks refused to give up her seat. Who else in the text refused to do something?	*The people in the boycott refused to back down. They refused to ride the buses.*

Dictionary

Read each word aloud.
Look at the picture or read the definition.

segregated

Gandhi

arrested

Words	Definitions
injustice	something that is not fair
refused	to show that you don't want to do something
arrested	stopped or held because a person has broken a law
back down	to stop doing something; to change your mind
successful	having reached a goal
integrated	all together as equals

Write one sentence using two of the words.

_____

_____

King and the Bus Boycott

Martin Luther King, Jr., was born in Atlanta, Georgia, in 1929. During this time, black people and white people were segregated, or kept apart. Schools and other public places, like restaurants, had sections for black people and sections for white people. This was the law. Young Martin felt this law was wrong. He wanted everyone to be treated the same.

Martin loved to learn, and he was a good student. He went to college 3 years early, when he was only 15 years old. In college, King learned about Mahatma Gandhi. He was a peaceful man who helped the people of India. They were treated poorly by India's leaders. Indian people suffered injustice, just as black Americans did. But instead of fighting and yelling, Gandhi used words and actions. Dr. King wanted to follow the nonviolent methods used by Gandhi. Maybe these methods would help black Americans.

Dr. King giving a speech

In 1955, Dr. King found a way to use these nonviolent methods. It started when a black woman named Rosa Parks was riding a bus.

Dr. King leading a march

In Montgomery, Alabama, the buses were segregated. That meant she was supposed to give up her seat to a white person. One day, she refused to do that. She was arrested.

King was upset about Mrs. Parks' arrest. Dr. King led marches and organized a bus boycott. He asked black people to stop riding the buses. The boycott was supposed to last only one day, but it went on for 381 days! All this time, thousands of black people walked instead of taking the bus. The bus companies lost money. Many people tried to stop the boycott. But King and his followers would not back down.

The year-long boycott was successful. The law was changed. Buses were integrated, and black people started riding again. But this time, they sat wherever they wanted.

Use New Words

Complete each sentence using a word from the word box.
Then read each sentence aloud.

<table>
<tr><td colspan="3">**Word Box**</td></tr>
<tr><td>arrested</td><td>back down</td><td>injustice</td></tr>
<tr><td>integrated</td><td>refused</td><td>successful</td></tr>
</table>

1 When a person is arrested for no reason, it is an

_____.

2 The baby cried and _____ to go to sleep.

3 The police _____ the bank robber.

4 I cannot change her mind; she will not _____.

5 The plan did not work. It was not _____.

6 Our school is _____; all kinds of children
go there.

Answer Questions

Read and answer each question.

1 What kind of a leader was Gandhi?

   Ⓐ fearful

   Ⓑ peaceful

   Ⓒ loud

2 How long did the bus boycott last?

   Ⓐ 1 day

   Ⓑ 2 months

   Ⓒ 381 days

3 What was the result of the year-long bus boycott?

   Ⓐ The buses were refused.

   Ⓑ The buses were integrated.

   Ⓒ The buses were segregated.

4 Which word means the opposite of **segregated**?

   Ⓐ integrated

   Ⓑ arrested

   Ⓒ organized

5 How did Rosa Parks help black Americans?

_____

_____

Write About It

Graphic Organizer

The bus boycott is over!
Make a sign that tells black people they can ride the buses again.
Use words from the word box.

Word Box

boycott	bus	integrated
ride	seat	segregated

People Can Change the World

Topic: People Can Change the World
Big Question: Do I have the power to change the world?

Tie It Together

Use the script below to guide students in discussing the Big Question and what they have learned about the topic from the paired selections.

Questions	Sample Responses
What was the same about the way Chavez and King fought for change?	*They both used nonviolent methods, such as boycotts, to improve people's lives.*
What was different about Chavez and King?	*Chavez was born in Arizona and King was born in Georgia. They were fighting for different causes.*
What injustices did the farmworkers suffer?	*Workers were paid very little. They had to live in run-down camps without clean water.*
What injustices did black Americans suffer?	*Black Americans were segregated from everyone else. Public places, such as schools and restaurants, had sections for black people and white people.*
During the grape boycott, who stopped buying grapes?	*People all over the country stopped buying grapes.*
During the bus boycott, who stopped riding the buses?	*Black people stopped riding the buses in Montgomery, Alabama.*
Our Big Question was "Do I have the power to change the world?" How did "Chavez and the Grape Boycott" answer this question?	*In the selection "Chavez and the Grape Boycott," Cesar Chavez was just an ordinary man. He saw something he didn't like, and he took steps to change it.*
How did "King and the Bus Boycott" answer it?	*In the selection "King and the Bus Boycott," King was also an ordinary man, but many people followed him. That was how he was able to change laws.*

Name: _____

Plan Your Writing

Graphic Organizer

Chavez and King both used boycotts as nonviolent methods.
Write facts about the boycotts on the picket signs.

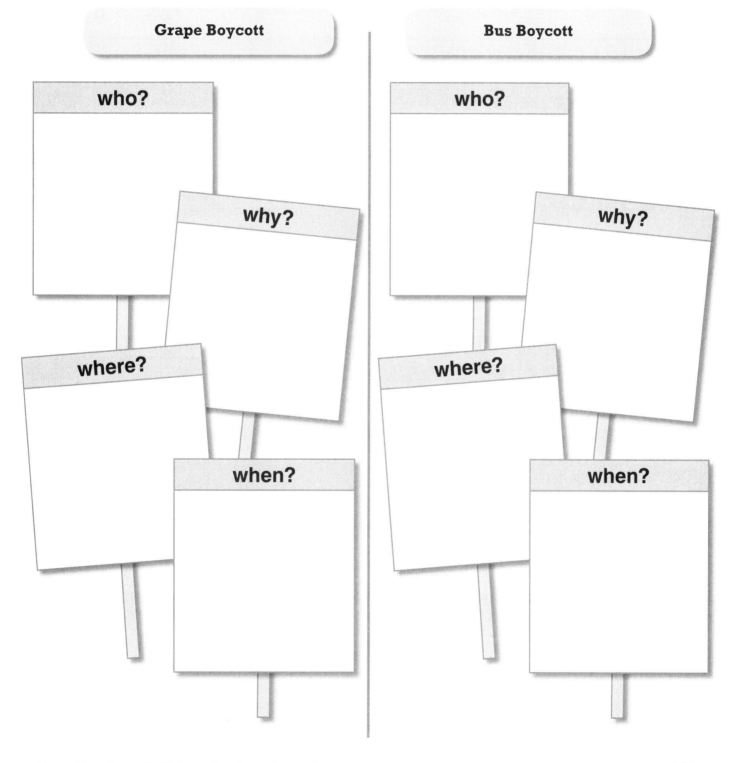

Grape Boycott

Bus Boycott

who?

why?

where?

when?

who?

why?

where?

when?

Write a Paragraph

Writing Prompt

Write a paragraph comparing the grape boycott and the bus boycott.

_____

_____

_____

_____

_____

_____

_____

_____

_____

_____

_____

_____

_____

Unit Overview
The First Railroad

Student Objective: Students will understand the impact that the transcontinental railroad had on the United States.

Big Question:

How did the transcontinental railroad change America?

Topic Introduction: Explain that the transcontinental railroad was built a long time ago. It linked people across the country. Tell students they will read two selections that tell more about the people affected by the railroad.

Paired Text Selections:

Selection: *Railroad Songs*
Nonfiction, Level K

Teacher Pages:

Selection: *Tracks Across America*
Nonfiction, Level M

Teacher Pages:

Assessment Materials:

Teacher Page: (Paired Text Discussion)

Student Pages: (Reproduce and distribute one copy to each student.)

Lesson Plan

1. Introduce the Selection

Ask students what they know about trains, and tell them how hard it must be to build a railroad. Tell students that they are going to read a story about workers who built America's first railroad, called the transcontinental railroad.

2. Learn New Vocabulary: Dictionary

Reproduce the Dictionary page and distribute it to each student. Read aloud each pictured word as you point to it. Have students echo you as they also point to each word. Ask students if they have ever seen a picture of the spikes on a porcupine, or someone with spiked hair. Also discuss different types of whistles, and what a train whistle might sound like. For defined vocabulary, read the definitions aloud. Have volunteers use each word in a sentence.

Have students write a sentence using two of the words. Then have students find each vocabulary word in the selection and read the context sentence.

3. Read the Selection

Reproduce the selection and distribute it to each student. Have students follow along silently as you read aloud. Direct students' attention to graphic elements or visual aids. Then have students read the selection independently, with a partner, or in small groups.

4. Apply Vocabulary: Use New Words

Reproduce the Use New Words page and distribute it to each student. Have students complete the activity independently, with a partner, or in small groups.

5. Analyze the Selection: Oral Close Reading Activity

Guide students in a discussion about the selection using the script on the following page. Explain that close reading will help them notice important parts of the selection. Encourage students to refer to the selection as necessary to find information.

To support visual learners, you may wish to cover up the sample responses and reproduce and distribute the discussion questions for students to refer to.

6. Understand the Selection: Answer Questions

Reproduce the Answer Questions page and distribute it to each student. Have students complete the activity. Encourage them to refer to the selection as necessary to help them answer questions and/or to check their answers.

You may wish to use this as a formative assessment to determine students' understanding of the text.

7. Write About the Selection: Write About It

Reproduce the Write About It page and distribute it to each student. Have students brainstorm in small groups and complete the writing assignment collaboratively or independently.

Oral Close Reading Activity

Ask students the following text-dependent questions and have them refer to the selection as necessary.

Questions	Sample Responses
Before trains, how did people travel?	by boat or by horse
How did trains make travel different?	Trains were faster than boats and horses. Trains didn't get hurt or tired.
What does it mean to ride the rails?	to ride on a train
How did you figure it out?	I read the sentences around those words. Those sentences talk about people riding trains.
Do you think working on the railroad was an easy job?	no
Why do you think that?	The men worked all the livelong day; they used a heavy tool, so they were tired; they had to work fast.
What is the first song about?	working all day long
In the line "Rise up so early in the morn," what does "morn" mean?	morning
How did you figure that out?	Workers normally get up early in the morning.
What does the second song talk about?	Workers are waiting for a train that is coming around the mountain.
Is this text fiction or nonfiction?	nonfiction
How do you know?	The text gives factual information about railroad songs.

Dictionary

Read each word aloud.
Look at the picture or read the definition.

tracks

spike

whistle

Words	Definitions
rails	tracks
pound	to hit very hard
folk songs	old music that everyone knows
livelong	whole; entire
crew	a group of workers
supplies	tools or other things that people need

Write one sentence using two of the words.

_____

_____

Railroad Songs

Railroads in America were built long ago, in the 1800s. Before trains, people traveled by boat or by horse. But rivers would freeze in winter, and horses would get hurt or tired. Trains changed all that. Trains were a new and fast way to travel. Everyone wanted to ride the rails.

Railroad tracks were built all across the country. Men worked hard to make the new tracks. They were told to do it fast. The men sang songs to help the work go faster. Men used a special tool to pound nails, or spikes, into the tracks. The tool was called a spike maul. The spike maul was very heavy. The men pounded all day. They sang railroad songs to forget how tired they were. Many of these songs became American folk songs. Here is one song that the men sang:

I've been working on the railroad
All the livelong day.
I've been working on the railroad
Just to pass the time away.
Can't you hear the whistle blowing?
Rise up so early in the morn!
Can't you hear the captain shouting:
"Dinah, blow your horn!"

Here is another song that the railroad workers sang:

 She'll be coming round the mountain when she comes.
She'll be coming round the mountain when she comes.
She'll be coming round the mountain,
She'll be coming round the mountain,
She'll be coming round the mountain when she comes.

Who do you think the song was about? No one really knows. But here's an idea. Ships and trains are sometimes thought of as women. Maybe "she" was a train. Maybe the crew hoped the train had food and supplies. Or maybe more workers were  coming. Now people sing this song in school or at camp. They may have other ideas of who the song is about.

There are many other railroad songs. They tell about the time of the trains. Back then, trains were the fastest way to travel. Now people are in more of a hurry. They travel by car or by plane. Many of the railroads are gone, but we still have the songs to remind us of that time.

Use New Words

Complete each sentence using a word from the word box.
Then read each sentence aloud.

Word Box

crew	folk	livelong
pound	rails	supplies

1 The train moved slowly on the _____.

2 We got pens and other school _____.

3 The building _____ did the work quickly.

4 The teacher read us a funny _____ tale.

5 Dad will _____ nails into the wood.

6 The baby cried all the _____ day.

Answer Questions

Read and answer each question.

1   What is a spike maul?

    Ⓐ a train that brings supplies

    Ⓑ a tool that pounds spikes

    Ⓒ a happy railroad song

2   Why did everyone want to ride the rails?

    Ⓐ Trains were new and fast.

    Ⓑ Trains were big and loud.

    Ⓒ People did not want to drive.

3   When workers sang "She'll Be Coming Round the Mountain" they probably felt _____.

    Ⓐ sadness

    Ⓑ hope

    Ⓒ fear

4   The second song is probably about a _____.

    Ⓐ train

    Ⓑ girl

    Ⓒ ship

5   What does the author mean by "the time of the trains"?

_____

_____

Write About It

Look at each picture. Think about the words to each song.
Write why the men sang it. Finish each sentence.
Use details from the text.

1 The men sang
"I've Been Working
on the Railroad"
because

_____

_____

_____

_____

_____

2 The men sang
"She'll Be Coming
Round the Mountain"
because

_____

_____

_____

_____

_____

Lesson Plan

1. **Introduce the Selection**

   Ask students about different modes of transportation, including the train. Then tell students that they are going to read about a historical event: the building of the transcontinental railroad, and how it changed the way Americans traveled.

2. **Learn New Vocabulary: Dictionary**

   Reproduce the Dictionary page and distribute it to each student. Read aloud each pictured word as you point to it. Have students echo you as they also point to each word. Have students point to the first picture. Tell them that the star shows San Francisco, which is on the West Coast. Explain that the second map shows New York City, which is on the East Coast, far from San Francisco. For defined vocabulary, read the definitions aloud. Have volunteers use each word in a sentence.

   Have students write a sentence using two of the words. Then have students find each vocabulary word in the selection and read the context sentence.

3. **Read the Selection**

   Reproduce the selection and distribute it to each student. Have students follow along silently as you read aloud. Direct students' attention to graphic elements or visual aids. Then have students read the selection independently, with a partner, or in small groups.

4. **Apply Vocabulary: Use New Words**

   Reproduce the Use New Words page and distribute it to each student. Have students complete the activity independently, with a partner, or in small groups.

5. **Analyze the Selection: Oral Close Reading Activity**

   Guide students in a discussion about the selection using the script on the following page. Explain that close reading will help them notice important parts of the selection. Encourage students to refer to the selection as necessary to find information.

   To support visual learners, you may wish to cover up the sample responses and reproduce and distribute the discussion questions for students to refer to.

6. **Understand the Selection: Answer Questions**

   Reproduce the Answer Questions page and distribute it to each student. Have students complete the activity. Encourage them to refer to the selection as necessary to help them answer questions and/or to check their answers.

   You may wish to use this as a formative assessment to determine students' understanding of the text.

7. **Write About the Selection: Write About It**

   Reproduce the Write About It page and distribute it to each student. Have students brainstorm in small groups and complete the writing assignment collaboratively or independently.

Oral Close Reading Activity

Ask students the following text-dependent questions and have them refer to the selection as necessary.

Questions	Sample Responses
Look at the map. Use your finger to trace along the ship route from New York City to San Francisco. Then use your finger to trace the train route. What do you notice?	*The train route is shorter.*
How did the railroad change what people could buy?	*People could buy things that came from far away.*
How did the Native Americans feel about the railroad?	*They did not like it.*
Why did they feel this way?	*The train cut through their land. The train passengers shot their buffalo.*
The Native Americans treated the buffalo differently than the train passengers did. What was the difference?	*Native Americans hunted buffalo for food. They only shot what they needed. The passengers shot too many of them.*
The author says the train helped people get to new places faster. How was this both good and bad?	*It was good for the people who wanted to explore and who wanted to sell things. It was bad for the Native Americans whose homes were destroyed.*
Is this selection fiction or nonfiction?	*nonfiction*
How do you know?	*The selection tells about an event in history.*

Name: _____

Dictionary

Read each word aloud.
Look at the picture or read the definition.

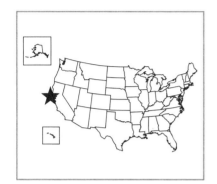

San Francisco

New York City

buffalo

Words	Definitions
transcontinental	crossing a continent
coast	land near the sea
affected	changed
expensive	costing a lot of money
destroyed	attacked; ruined
passengers	people who ride the train

Write one sentence using two of the words.

_____

_____

Tracks Across America

The transcontinental railroad was built between 1863 and 1869. It changed America forever. It linked the West Coast and the East Coast. The railroad affected many people.

For some people, the railroad was good. Store owners could trade with people far away. They could buy and sell things like fruit, animals, and steel. Before, people traveled from San Francisco to New York City by ship. It took many months and lots of money. By train, it took only three days and not as much money. Thanks to the railroad, trade and travel were faster and less expensive.

New York City

San Francisco

Key

For other people, the railroad was bad. Native Americans called the train "the iron horse" because now people were riding trains instead of horses. Native Americans did not like the train. Train tracks cut through their land. Trains destroyed their homes. Train passengers destroyed their food. Native Americans hunted buffalo for food. They only hunted what they needed. There were many buffalo. Then train passengers began shooting the buffalo. In a few years, most of the buffalo were gone.

Native Americans fought back. In the end, though, the railroad won. Native Americans lost their land and their way of life.

The railroad changed the land and the people. For some people, it was a good change. For others, it was not.

Use New Words

Complete each sentence using a word from the word box.
Then read each sentence aloud.

Word Box

affected	coast	destroyed
expensive	passengers	transcontinental

1 The movie star has three _____ cars.

2 The tornado _____ half the town.

3 The _____ railroad linked the West Coast and the East Coast.

4 All _____ must wear a seat belt in the car.

5 I can hear the ocean waves on the _____.

6 My tight shoes _____ how I walked.

Answer Questions

Read and answer each question.

1 How long did it take to build the transcontinental railroad?

Ⓐ ten years

Ⓑ six years

Ⓒ six months

2 Which words from the text tell what **trade** means?

Ⓐ buy and sell things

Ⓑ less expensive

Ⓒ there were many buffalo

3 The train was called "the iron horse" because _____.

Ⓐ a horse was better than a train

Ⓑ the iron train was as fast as a horse

Ⓒ people rode trains instead of horses

4 Who enjoyed the railroad most?

Ⓐ passengers

Ⓑ Native Americans

Ⓒ railroad workers

5 Why was it called the transcontinental railroad?

_____

_____

Write About It

Graphic Organizer

Pretend it is 1869.
Make a sign for a train ride from San Francisco to New York City.
Write why people should ride the train and not go by ship.
Use details from the text.

The First Railroad

Topic: The First Railroad
Big Question: How did the transcontinental railroad change America?

Tie It Together

Use the script below to guide students in discussing the Big Question and what they have learned about the topic from the paired selections.

Questions	Sample Responses
The transcontinental railroad changed the lives of many people. According to the selections, who were these people?	*railroad workers, train passengers, Native Americans*
Who sang railroad songs? Why did they sing?	*Railroad workers sang these songs to make the time go by faster and to forget how tired they were.*
In "Tracks Across America," which two groups did not agree about the railroad? Explain your answer.	*The passengers and the Native Americans did not agree. The passengers thought the railroad was good because it helped them travel faster and for less money. The Native Americans thought the railroad was bad because it destroyed their land.*
In "Railroad Songs," how do the photos help you understand the text?	*The photos show what the railroad songs are about. One photo shows the railroad workers.*
In "Tracks Across America," how does the map help you understand the text?	*The map shows the long ocean route from New York City to San Francisco. It also shows the train route.*
Our Big Question was "How did the transcontinental railroad change America?" After reading both selections, what is your answer to this question?	*The railroad changed America because now people could travel farther for less money. It also changed the way America looked, because the railroad cut through mountains and other areas of land.*

Name: _____

Plan Your Writing

How did the railroad affect the workers?
What about the passengers? And the Native Americans?
Write your ideas in the smoke clouds.

workers

passengers

Native Americans

Write a Paragraph

The texts are about workers, passengers, and Native Americans. Write how each group felt about the train. Use words from the word box.

Word Box

angry	happy	hopeful	lucky
sad	scared	tired	

_____

_____

_____

_____

_____

_____

_____

_____

_____

_____

_____

Community Art

Student Objective: Students will understand the significance that art has on the community.

Big Question:

How is a community like a puzzle?

Topic Introduction: Explain that all members of a community bring something special to that community. They are the pieces of the puzzle. Tell students they will read selections about outdoor art that honors the people of two communities. Each form of art is made up of small pieces, as well.

Paired Text Selections:

Selection: *Farm Art*
        Nonfiction, Level M

Teacher Pages:

Student Pages:

Selection: *Wall of Welcome*
        Nonfiction, Level M

Teacher Pages:

Student Pages:

Assessment Materials:

Teacher Page: (Paired Text Discussion)

Student Pages: (Reproduce and distribute one copy to each student.)

Lesson Plan

1. **Introduce the Selection**

   Have students think about any murals or community art in your area. Who created them? What do they represent? Tell students that they are going to read a story about a California artist who makes huge pieces of roadside art. People enjoy seeing the artwork as they drive by.

2. **Learn New Vocabulary: Dictionary**

   Reproduce the Dictionary page and distribute it to each student. Read aloud each pictured word as you point to it. Have students echo you as they also point to each word. For defined vocabulary, read the definitions aloud. Have volunteers use each word in a sentence. Point out that *workshop* and *landscape* are compound words. They are made of two smaller words.

   Have students write a sentence using two of the words. Then have students find each vocabulary word in the selection and read the context sentence.

3. **Read the Selection**

   Reproduce the selection and distribute it to each student. Have students follow along silently as you read aloud. Direct students' attention to graphic elements or visual aids. Then have students read the selection independently, with a partner, or in small groups.

4. **Apply Vocabulary: Use New Words**

   Reproduce the Use New Words page and distribute it to each student. Have students complete the activity independently, with a partner, or in small groups.

5. **Analyze the Selection: Oral Close Reading Activity**

   Guide students in a discussion about the selection using the script on the following page. Explain that close reading will help them notice important parts of the selection. Encourage students to refer to the selection as necessary to find information.

   To support visual learners, you may wish to cover up the sample responses and reproduce and distribute the discussion questions for students to refer to.

6. **Understand the Selection: Answer Questions**

   Reproduce the Answer Questions page and distribute it to each student. Have students complete the activity. Encourage them to refer to the selection as necessary to help them answer questions and/or to check their answers.

   You may wish to use this as a formative assessment to determine students' understanding of the text.

7. **Write About the Selection: Write About It**

   Reproduce the Write About It page and distribute it to each student. Have students brainstorm in small groups and complete the writing assignment collaboratively or independently.

Oral Close Reading Activity

Ask students the following text-dependent questions and have them refer to the selection as necessary.

Questions	Sample Responses
In the first paragraph, what does the word "greens" mean?	*green leafy vegetables*
How can you tell?	*because the author is talking about lettuce and salad*
Where does John Cerney live?	*Salinas, California*
How do you know?	*The first sentence talks about Salinas, California. The author says Cerney is a local artist, and a local is a person who lives in that area.*
Who are the people shown in the lettuce field?	*people who used to work on the farm*
Why are the figures there?	*The farmer wanted to show the community that it takes a lot of people to grow food.*
What are the figures made of?	*They are made of thin plywood.*
Cerney's artwork may only last a few years. How does he feel about this?	*He thinks it's okay because they are still in books and pictures.*
How do the photos help you with the text?	*I can see how big the figures are. In one picture, I can see the pieces of the finished artwork, and how it is like a puzzle.*

Dictionary

Read each word aloud.
Look at the picture or read the definition.

lettuce

field

plywood

Words	Definitions
workshop	a room where an artist works
model	a person that an artist paints or draws
locals	people who live in an area
tourists	people visiting an area
landscape	a pretty view of the land

Write one sentence using two of the words.

_____

_____

Farm Art

As you drive through Salinas, California, you will see lettuce, lettuce, and more lettuce. That's because Salinas grows most of the country's salad greens. Look out the window, and you pass one field after another. Lots of workers are in the fields, bending over, cutting lettuce. Others are packing the lettuce in boxes. They all look so busy. Wait! Did you see that? Are those giant people in that field?

Yes, they are giant people. They are 18 feet tall! The figures are in the middle of a farm. They show real people who once worked there. The farm owner wanted to show the community that it takes a lot of people to grow food. We see lettuce piled up neatly at the grocery store. But we hardly think of all the people who get the lettuce from the farm to our table.

The workers are an important part of the farm and of the community. That's why the farm owner asked John Cerney, a local artist, to find a way to honor the workers.

Farmers and business people love Cerney's work. His workshop is a busy place. Cerney starts with an idea. He takes many photos of the person who is the model. He studies the photos and finds the perfect one. Then he draws the person on small, thin pieces of plywood.

He doesn't see the whole piece of art until later. He puts the pieces together outside, like a giant puzzle. When it's all put together, he stands back and looks up at his work. Up close, you can see the puzzle pieces. But when you're zooming by in a car, you see a huge person that you didn't expect to see.

Since the artwork is done on thin sheets of plywood, the sun, wind, and rain wear down the wood. So the figures may only last six or seven years. Cerney already has had to redo several of his giant people. "They won't last forever. Only in books and pictures, but that's okay," says Cerney.

Locals and tourists enjoy the giant outdoor art. It is part of the landscape.

This giant cut-out is 40 feet long. It is made of 550 plywood pieces that Cerney painted. Then he put them together like a puzzle.

Use New Words

Complete each sentence using a word from the word box.
Then read each sentence aloud.

Word Box

landscape	locals	model
plywood	tourists	workshop

1 The artist asked the _____ to sit still as he painted her.

2 In the summer, the _____ has a lot of flowers.

3 The kitchen cabinets are made of _____.

4 The _____ are visiting here from Japan.

5 The carpenter's _____ is filled with tools.

6 We were born here, so we are _____.

Answer Questions

Read and answer each question.

1 Which words tell about plywood?

   Ⓐ thick poles of wood

   Ⓑ thin sheets of wood

   Ⓒ light disks of wood

2 What is another word for **tourist**?

   Ⓐ farmer

   Ⓑ local

   Ⓒ visitor

3 Which sentence uses **figure** in the same way as the story?

   Ⓐ I can't figure out the answer.

   Ⓑ A triangle is a figure with three sides.

   Ⓒ The artist made a figure of a cat.

4 Why don't the cut-out figures last long?

   Ⓐ They wear down because they are outside.

   Ⓑ The owners tear them down to buy new ones.

   Ⓒ The artist lets people have them for a short time.

5 In what way is each cut-out figure like a puzzle?

_____

_____

Name: _____

Write About It

Graphic Organizer

In the paint spots, write the steps John Cerney takes to create his art.

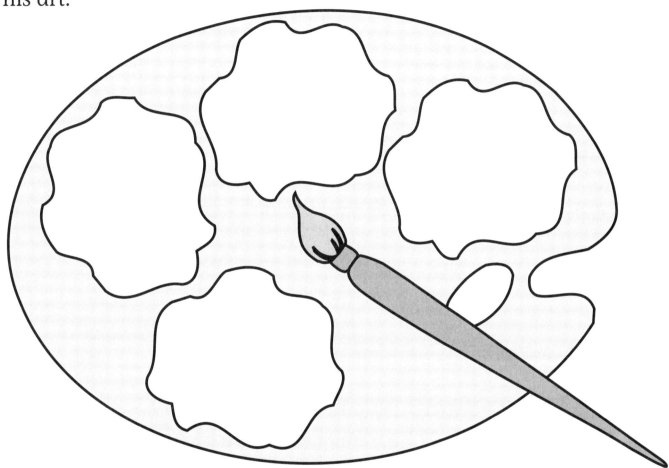

Writing Prompt

Write a paragraph to tell how John Cerney creates his art. Use the graphic organizer to help you.

_____

_____

_____

_____

Lesson Plan

1. **Introduce the Selection**

   Have students imagine what a plain brick wall looks like. Then tell students that they are going to read a nonfiction selection about a plain brick wall that community members turned into a beautiful work of art.

2. **Learn New Vocabulary: Dictionary**

   Reproduce the Dictionary page and distribute it to each student. Read aloud each pictured word as you point to it. Have students echo you as they also point to each word. For defined vocabulary, read the definitions aloud. Have volunteers use each word in a sentence. Guide students in identifying the noun that names a person. (volunteer) Then have them identify the noun that names a place. (neighborhood)

   Have students write a sentence using two of the words. Then have students find each vocabulary word in the selection and read the context sentence.

3. **Read the Selection**

   Reproduce the selection and distribute it to each student. Have students follow along silently as you read aloud. Direct students' attention to graphic elements or visual aids. Then have students read the selection independently, with a partner, or in small groups.

4. **Apply Vocabulary: Use New Words**

   Reproduce the Use New Words page and distribute it to each student. Have students complete the activity independently, with a partner, or in small groups.

5. **Analyze the Selection: Oral Close Reading Activity**

   Guide students in a discussion about the selection using the script on the following page. Explain that close reading will help them notice important parts of the selection. Encourage students to refer to the selection as necessary to find information.

   To support visual learners, you may wish to cover up the sample responses and reproduce and distribute the discussion questions for students to refer to.

6. **Understand the Selection: Answer Questions**

   Reproduce the Answer Questions page and distribute it to each student. Have students complete the activity. Encourage them to refer to the selection as necessary to help them answer questions and/or to check their answers.

   You may wish to use this as a formative assessment to determine students' understanding of the text.

7. **Write About the Selection: Write About It**

   Reproduce the Write About It page and distribute it to each student. Have students brainstorm in small groups and complete the writing assignment collaboratively or independently.

Oral Close Reading Activity

Ask students the following text-dependent questions and have them refer to the selection as necessary.

Questions	Sample Responses
Where is the Wall of Welcome?	*Austin, Texas*
What does the wall's name tell you about its purpose?	*It welcomes shoppers to the shopping center and to the neighborhood.*
How did Jean Graham get the wall project started?	*She gave classes to teach people how to make mosaics.*
What are mosaics?	*pictures made with chips of glass or clay*
What are some of the different tiles like?	*Schools, families, and businesses made tiles to show what they loved about the neighborhood. Some have words that tell about the history of the neighborhood.*
How long did it take to complete the wall?	*five years*
What does it mean to "walk the wall"?	*to walk along the wall slowly, carefully looking at each detail*
How did you figure this out?	*Some people drive by quickly and can't see the details. The details of the wall can only be seen when someone is up close, walking from one end to the other.*
How do the photos help you with the text?	*I can see someone making a tile and I can see what the finished tile looks like. I can see part of the finished wall. Now I know what a mosaic looks like.*

Name: _____

Dictionary

Read each word aloud.
Look at the picture or read the definition.

mosaics

neighborhood

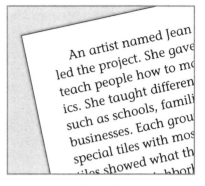

text

Words	Definitions
welcome	a happy greeting
collected	brought together
memories	things you remember from the past
details	small parts of something big
volunteer	a person who helps out for free

Write one sentence using two of the words.

_____

_____

Wall of Welcome

Visit the Crestview Shopping Center in Austin, Texas, and you will get a big welcome. A big Wall of Welcome, that is! The wall by the shopping center was once just plain brick. The community wanted the wall to welcome shoppers. They wanted it to be beautiful. So they covered the brick wall with mosaics. Mosaics are pictures made with chips of colored glass or clay.

An artist named Jean Graham led the project. She gave classes to teach people how to make mosaics. She taught different groups, such as schools, families, and businesses. Each group made special tiles with mosaics. Their tiles showed what they loved about the neighborhood. These neighborhood tiles were placed all along the top of the wall.

Next, it was time to make the main part of the wall. People collected photos and told stories about the neighborhood. These memories gave people ideas. The artist made a small drawing of each idea. Then she made the tiles for the main part. Finally, many people put the tiles on the wall. It took five years. When the wall was finished, they named it the Wall of Welcome.

People enjoy the Wall of Welcome from far away as they drive by in their cars. But the details can only be seen up close. People "walk the wall" and read the tiny text. Some tiles have words that tell facts about the neighborhood. These tiles, along with the picture tiles, tell the history of the neighborhood.

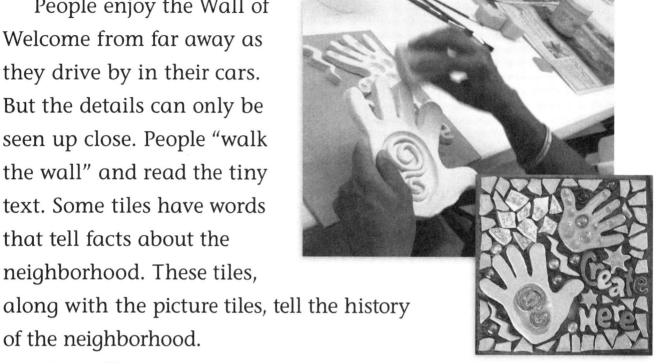

The wall has been good for the community. People proudly point out the tiles they made. Visitors from out of town come to see the wall. Other groups want to know how to make their own neighborhood wall. One volunteer who worked on the wall said each person is like a mosaic piece. Each one is different, but together, they are part of a greater picture.

Use New Words

Complete each sentence using a word from the word box.
Then read each sentence aloud.

Word Box

collected	details	memories
neighborhood	volunteer	welcome

1 I know the main idea, but I can't remember the _____.

2 My grandmother died when I was little. I don't have any

_____ of her.

3 I live in a quiet _____ with lots of trees.

4 Aunt Mary gave me a warm _____ when I visited.

5 I _____ the walnuts that fell from the tree.

6 I am a _____ at the school.

Answer Questions

Read and answer each question.

1 Which words tell about a mosaic?

    Ⓐ chips of colored clay

    Ⓑ smooth blue tile

    Ⓒ shiny stones

2 Who is Jean Graham?

    Ⓐ a shopper

    Ⓑ an artist

    Ⓒ a visitor

3 What is another word for **neighborhood**?

    Ⓐ volunteers

    Ⓑ school

    Ⓒ community

4 Look at the flying pig on the wall. What does its sign say?

    Ⓐ Welcome to the Neighborhood

    Ⓑ Welcome to Crestview

    Ⓒ Welcome to Austin

5 In what way are the community members like mosaic pieces?

_____

_____

Write About It

Imagine you are Jean Graham.
Tell people your ideas for the plain brick wall.
Write your ideas around the center tile.

Wall of Welcome

Write a paragraph about your ideas.

_____

_____

_____

_____

_____

Community Art

Topic: Community Art
Big Question: How is a community like a puzzle?

Tie It Together

Use the script below to guide students in discussing the Big Question and what they have learned about the topic from the paired selections.

Questions	Sample Responses
What is the same about the artists in the selections?	*They both use small pieces to make big art. They both make their communities more beautiful.*
What is different about the artists?	*Cerney works mostly alone; Graham needs volunteers. Cerney is in California; Graham is in Texas. They use different materials.*
According to the selections, what did both artists use to create their art?	*They both used photographs.*
How are Graham's mosaics similar to Cerney's puzzle pieces?	*Graham's mosaics are like puzzle pieces too. Together, the mosaics make a big picture.*
Our Big Question was "How is a community like a puzzle?" How did the selection "Farm Art" answer this question?	*In "Farm Art," individual farmworkers are the smaller pieces of the farming community.*
How did "Wall of Welcome" answer the Big Question?	*In "Wall of Welcome," community members are the smaller pieces of the whole community.*

Plan Your Writing

Cerney and Graham are well-known artists in their communities.
Fill out the chart to tell about them.

	Farm Art	Wall of Welcome
Who is the artist?		
Why did the artist make it?		
What is the art made of?		
What does it show?		
How does the community feel about the art?		

Write a Paragraph

Writing Prompt

Write a paragraph comparing Cerney and Graham. Talk about their art.

_____

_____

_____

_____

_____

_____

_____

_____

_____

_____

_____

_____

_____

Answer Key

TE = Teacher's Edition
SB = Student Book

Parts of a Plant

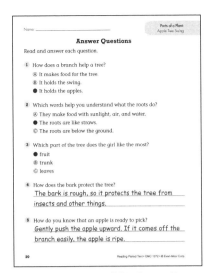

TE Page 19 / SB Page 6

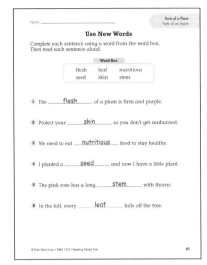

TE Page 20 / SB Page 7

TE Page 27 / SB Page 12

TE Page 28 / SB Page 13

Simple Machines Help Us

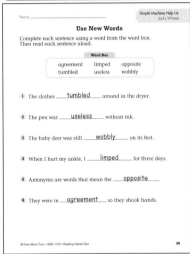

TE Page 39 / SB Page 22

TE Page 40 / SB Page 23

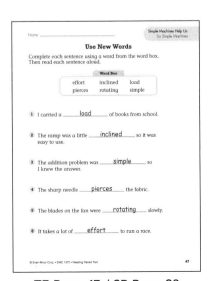

TE Page 47 / SB Page 28

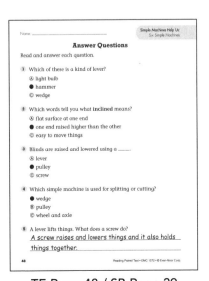

TE Page 48 / SB Page 29

Understanding Magnets

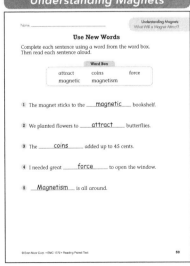

TE Page 59 / SB Page 38

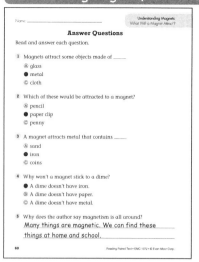

Answer Questions

Read and answer each question.

1. Magnets attract some objects made of ___.
   - Ⓐ glass
   - ● metal
   - Ⓒ cloth

2. Which of these would be attracted to a magnet?
   - Ⓐ pencil
   - ● paper clip
   - Ⓒ penny

3. A magnet attracts metal that contains ___.
   - Ⓐ sand
   - ● iron
   - Ⓒ coins

4. Why won't a magnet stick to a dime?
   - ● A dime doesn't have iron.
   - Ⓑ A dime doesn't have paper.
   - Ⓒ A dime doesn't have metal.

5. Why does the author say magnetism is all around?
   Many things are magnetic. We can find these
   things at home and school.

TE Page 60 / SB Page 39

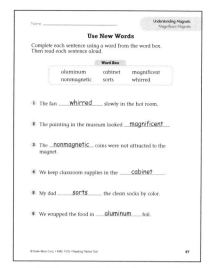

Use New Words

Complete each sentence using a word from the word box.
Then read each sentence aloud.

Word Box

| aluminum | cabinet | magnificent |
| nonmagnetic | sorts | whirred |

1. The fan __whirred__ slowly in the hot room.

2. The painting in the museum looked __magnificent__.

3. The __nonmagnetic__ coins were not attracted to the magnet.

4. We keep classroom supplies in the __cabinet__.

5. My dad __sorts__ the clean socks by color.

6. We wrapped the food in __aluminum__ foil.

TE Page 67 / SB Page 44

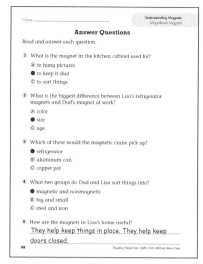

Answer Questions

Read and answer each question.

1. What is the magnet in the kitchen cabinet used for?
   - Ⓐ to hang pictures
   - ● to keep it shut
   - Ⓒ to sort things

2. What is the biggest difference between Lisa's refrigerator magnets and Dad's magnet at work?
   - Ⓐ color
   - ● size
   - Ⓒ age

3. Which of these would the magnetic crane pick up?
   - ● refrigerator
   - Ⓑ aluminum can
   - Ⓒ copper pot

4. What two groups do Dad and Lisa sort things into?
   - ● magnetic and nonmagnetic
   - Ⓑ big and small
   - Ⓒ steel and iron

5. How are the magnets in Lisa's home useful?
   They help keep things in place. They help keep
   doors closed.

TE Page 68 / SB Page 45

We Help Each Other

Use New Words

Complete each sentence using a word from the word box.
Then read each sentence aloud.

Word Box

| answer | donate | eyed |
| generous | luckily | stingy |

1. Kim is so __stingy__. She wouldn't let me have part of her lunch.

2. My sister is __generous__. She always shares her food.

3. I let the phone ring three times, then I __answer__ it.

4. __Luckily__, it stopped raining by noon.

5. We can __donate__ some of our toys to the children.

6. I __eyed__ the red bird until it flew away.

TE Page 79 / SB Page 54

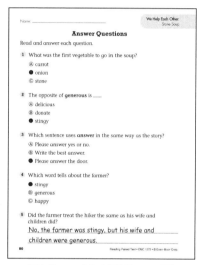

Answer Questions

Read and answer each question.

1. What was the first vegetable to go in the soup?
   - Ⓐ carrot
   - ● onion
   - Ⓒ stone

2. The opposite of **generous** is ___.
   - Ⓐ delicious
   - Ⓑ donate
   - ● stingy

3. Which sentence uses **answer** in the same way as the story?
   - Ⓐ Please answer yes or no.
   - Ⓑ Write the best answer.
   - ● Please answer the door.

4. Which word tells about the farmer?
   - ● stingy
   - Ⓑ generous
   - Ⓒ happy

5. Did the farmer treat the hiker the same as his wife and children did?
   No, the farmer was stingy, but his wife and
   children were generous.

TE Page 80 / SB Page 55

Use New Words

Complete each sentence using a word from the word box.
Then read each sentence aloud.

Word Box

| capture | exchange | feast |
| littered | reception | spectators |

1. Papers fell out of the bag and __littered__ the street.

2. The __spectators__ all clapped for the winner.

3. The wedding __reception__ was in a garden.

4. The mice had a __feast__ with the extra food.

5. The pants were too small, so the store gave us an __exchange__ for a bigger size.

6. I tried to __capture__ the butterfly with my net.

TE Page 87 / SB Page 60

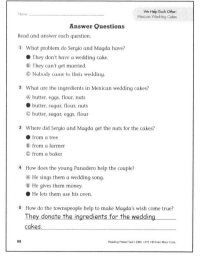

Answer Questions

Read and answer each question.

1. What problem do Sergio and Magda have?
   - ● They don't have a wedding cake.
   - Ⓑ They can't get married.
   - Ⓒ Nobody came to their wedding.

2. What are the ingredients in Mexican wedding cakes?
   - Ⓐ butter, eggs, flour, nuts
   - ● butter, sugar, flour, nuts
   - Ⓒ butter, sugar, eggs, flour

3. Where did Sergio and Magda get the nuts for the cakes?
   - ● from a tree
   - Ⓑ from a farmer
   - Ⓒ from a baker

4. How does the young Panadero help the couple?
   - Ⓐ He sings them a wedding song.
   - Ⓑ He gives them money.
   - ● He lets them use his oven.

5. How do the townspeople help to make Magda's wish come true?
   They donate the ingredients for the wedding
   cakes.

TE Page 88 / SB Page 61

National Memorials

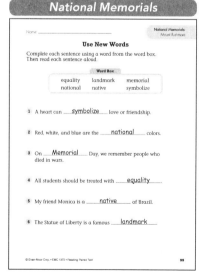

Use New Words

Complete each sentence using a word from the word box.
Then read each sentence aloud.

Word Box

| equality | landmark | memorial |
| national | native | symbolize |

1. A heart can __symbolize__ love or friendship.

2. Red, white, and blue are the __national__ colors.

3. On __Memorial__ Day, we remember people who died in wars.

4. All students should be treated with __equality__.

5. My friend Monica is a __native__ of Brazil.

6. The Statue of Liberty is a famous __landmark__.

TE Page 99 / SB Page 70

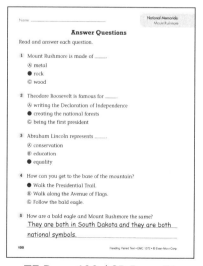

Answer Questions

Read and answer each question.

1. Mount Rushmore is made of ___.
   - Ⓐ metal
   - ● rock
   - Ⓒ wood

2. Theodore Roosevelt is famous for ___.
   - Ⓐ writing the Declaration of Independence
   - ● creating the national forests
   - Ⓒ being the first president

3. Abraham Lincoln represents ___.
   - Ⓐ conservation
   - Ⓑ education
   - ● equality

4. How can you get to the base of the mountain?
   - ● Walk the Presidential Trail.
   - Ⓑ Walk along the Avenue of Flags.
   - Ⓒ Follow the bald eagle.

5. How are a bald eagle and Mount Rushmore the same?
   They are both in South Dakota and they are both
   national symbols.

TE Page 100 / SB Page 71

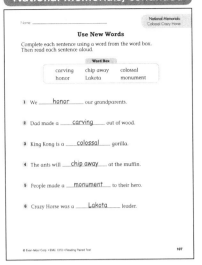

TE Page 107 / SB Page 76

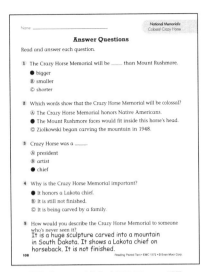

TE Page 108 / SB Page 77

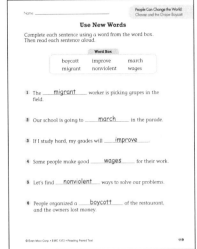

TE Page 119 / SB Page 86

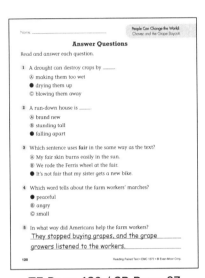

TE Page 120 / SB Page 87

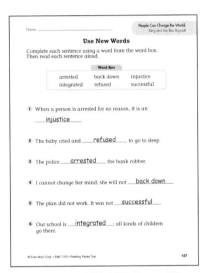

TE Page 127 / SB Page 92

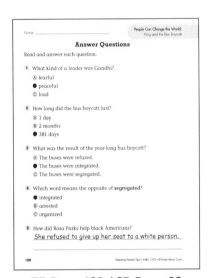

TE Page 128 / SB Page 93

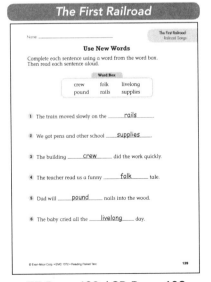

TE Page 139 / SB Page 102

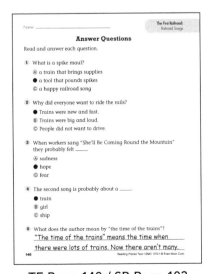

TE Page 140 / SB Page 103

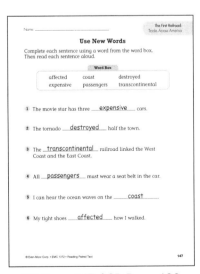

TE Page 147 / SB Page 108

175

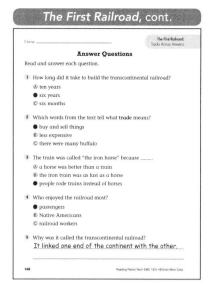

TE Page 148 / SB Page 109

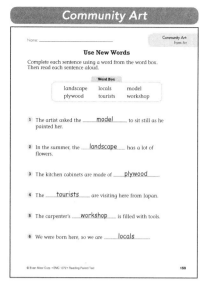

TE Page 159 / SB Page 118

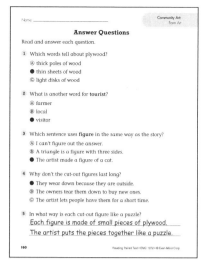

TE Page 160 / SB Page 119

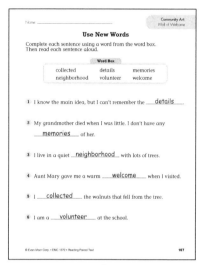

TE Page 167 / SB Page 124

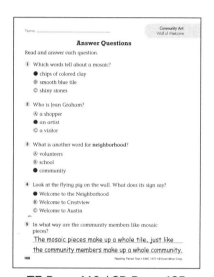

TE Page 168 / SB Page 125